The Handprinted Books
of Leonard and Virginia Woolf
at the Hogarth Press, 1917-1932

Studies in Modern Literature, No. 52

A. Walton Litz, General Series Editor

Professor of English
Princeton University

Carolyn G. Heilbrun

Consulting Editor for Titles on Virginia Woolf
Professor of English
Columbia University

Daniel Mark Fogel

Consulting Editor for Titles on Henry James
Professor of English
Louisiana State University
Editor, The Henry James Review

Other Titles in This Series

The Handprinted Books of Leonard and Virginia Woolf at the Hogarth Press, 1917-1932

by
Donna E. Rhein

UMI RESEARCH PRESS
Ann Arbor, Michigan

Produced and distributed by
UMI Research Press
an imprint of
University Microfilms International
A Xerox Information Resources Company
Ann Arbor, Michigan 48106

Library of Congress Cataloging in Publication Data

Rhein, Donna E. (Donna Elizabeth), 1943-
The handprinted books of Leonard and Virginia
Woolf at the Hogarth Press, 1917-1932.

(Studies in modern literature ; no. 52)
Bibliography: p.
Includes index.
1. Hogarth Press.   2. Hand-printed books—Bibliography—Catalogs.   3. Hand-printed books—Publishing.
4. Private presses—Great Britain—History—20th
century.   5. Woolf, Leonard, 1880-1969—Biography.
6. Woolf, Virginia, 1882-1941—Biography.   7. English
literature—20th century—Publishing.   8. Authors,
English—20th century—Biography.   9. Printers—Great
Britain—Biography.   10. Printing—England—History—
20th century.   11. Publishers and publishing—England—
History—20th century.   12. Handpress.   I. Title.
II. Series.
Z232.H73R47   1985   070.5'092'2 [B]   85-14144
ISBN 0-8357-1694-5 (alk. paper)

For Merritt Betts

Contents

List of Illustrations

Preface

I have been interested in the Woolfs and their Hogarth Press since reading Leonard's autobiography *Beginning Again* in the early 1960s. My original intent was to focus my study on the illustrators, but when I discussed this project with Quentin Bell and others in England in 1970, I discovered that information would be scarce. I also learned that J. Howard Woolmer was making a checklist of the Press for the period of Virginia's partnership, which ended in 1938, and that Mary Gaither was adding an introduction outlining the history of the Press. This work has been published and has proved invaluable to rare bookmen and researchers alike for standard details on the books. Stanley Olsen has finished but not published a dissertation for the University of London on several authors printed and published during the Press's early years. It is a very useful source for information on the early history but makes no pretense at interest in the technical side of the Press even though Olsen emphasizes the importance of the Press to the Woolfs in its formative years. It is also the earliest written work on the Press by someone not directly involved with it. Among those directly involved with the Press, both the Woolfs and John Lehmann have written about it. For information on the Woolfs as well as insights into their relationship to the Press, Quentin Bell's biography of his aunt, Virginia Woolf, and a joint biography of Leonard and Virginia by two people well known to Leonard and to publishing, George Spater and Ian Parsons, provide solid information. Spater was the cataloguer for Leonard's papers, which were given to the University of Sussex at his death in 1969. Ian Parsons, long an editor with Chatto and Windus and a neighbor of Leonard's, was instrumental in arranging for the merger of the Hogarth Press and his firm in 1964; his wife was Leonard's literary executrix.

The present study, which attempts to show through the handprinted books the rich and fascinating contribution made by the Woolfs to British literature and their place in the tradition of the book arts, would not have been completed without help from many individuals. The curiosity and support of several friends and colleagues and the encouragement of Dr. Gwen Raaberg and the late Robert Plant Armstrong at the University of Texas at Dallas have been vital. Nor would it have been possible to write this book without the interest and assistance of several special librarians and their staffs: Lola L. Szladits, the Berg Collection at the New York Public Library; James Davis, Special Collections at the University of California at Los Angeles; Decherd Turner, the Humanities Research Center at the University of Texas at Austin; and Leila Luedeking, Special Collections at Washington State University. A very special thanks goes to William Cagle and David Warrington of the Lilly Library at Indiana University for making their collection of the handprinted books, which includes at least one example of each title, available to me and for making the arrangements for the illustrations in this book which add so much to an understanding of what the Woolfs accomplished at the Hogarth Press. All the photographs are courtesy of the Lilly Library, Indiana University, Bloomington, Indiana. Chatto and Windus has kindly given permission, on behalf of the Hogarth Press, for these reproductions.

Introduction

Leonard and Virginia Woolf printed and published thirty-four books between the years 1917 and 1932. They chose works, written by themselves or friends and acquaintances, of poetry, fiction and essay which might not have been published otherwise. Perhaps the material was too slight in form and content to meet the criteria of the marketplace or the authors were unknown and their talents untried. Anyone with a general knowledge of twentieth-century literature will recognize today the poets T.S. Eliot, John Crowe Ransom and Robert Graves from the list of authors published by the Woolfs during these fifteen years. And some familiarity with the Woolfs' circle of friends will make finding Clive Bell, Roger Fry, E.M. Forster and Vita Sackville-West among these other names seem quite natural. But there are some names with no obvious connection to the Woolfs' public or private lives. This is puzzling because they spent a great deal of time and effort printing books to give these people recognition: poets such as Herbert E. Palmer, Stanley Snaith, Frank Prewitt and Ena Limebeer. This meant quite literally hours of physical labor, with the Woolfs (willingly) working at their "hobby" most weekday afternoons. Many critics do not yet understand the role the Hogarth Press played in the lives of the Woolfs in spite of the mass of material written about Virginia and the availability of Leonard's autobiographies. It is a shock to realize that Virginia wrote not only her major works of fiction during the 1920s but also scores of reviews and essays. At this same time, Leonard was active not only as an author but also as a literary and political editor and a contributor to several journals. He worked steadily for the Labour Party as a resource person for colonial affairs as well. It has been said by Leonard and nearly all who knew them well that each Woolf worked very hard at three full-time jobs throughout their married life. The Hogarth Press was certainly one of these jobs.

As yet, little has been written about the Press concerning its place among the adventurous publishing houses of the twentieth century in terms of who was published, and how authors were chosen by the Woolfs in the first place.

Though most of the Press' records were lost during the Second World War, all the existing private papers are available to scholars. A great deal has been written about Virginia's place in English literature, but little mention is made of her role as a partner in the Hogarth Press. Her diaries and letters, however, are a major resource for learning about her reactions and thoughts on this hobby which kept evolving into a responsibility. Fortunately, Leonard has told his story of the Press in his autobiographies, where it can be seen as a thread weaving the Woolfs' lives together as it provided a means for creative freedom and financial stability. The Hogarth Press emerges from the Woolfs' writing as a mixed blessing, one which developed a will of its own, and, on occasion, caused the Woolfs enormous frustration. It proved itself, however, to be an appropriate venture for two writers as it happily joined a shared hobby, printing, with the ideal publishing situation for an author: control over the publisher.

The purpose of this study is to give an annotated bibliography of the books and discuss the authors whose words were handprinted by the Woolfs. It has proved easiest to investigate the books and understand how their authors came to be connected with the Press by considering them in groups based on their relationship to the Woolfs. Of course the Woolfs printed their own work and that of friends. They also printed work by people they admired and wanted to encourage in their endeavor to reach the public eye. Since most of these people developed careers of some note, it is possible to give an indication of their relationship to the Woolfs and what these particular books meant to them at the time of publication. They or their associates from this period of literature between the wars in England were articulate people and most wrote their impressions and opinions sometimes for a private and often for a public audience. Although many of them have died, there is a vivid trail of letters, memories and critical essays leading the curious present generation to their views. There are also a few authors in this study, referred to as "worthy unknowns," about whom little is known or for whom it is difficult to determine why the Woolfs cared to give their careers a boost.

Books are physical objects of sensual as well as intellectual interest. When they are made by hand, they necessarily reveal something of the maker. As much as some might wish to ignore the Woolfs' hands while considering how well their minds worked when they selected the matter of these books, it is not possible with the unique handprinted products of the Hogarth Press. The Woolfs knew full well the long tradition of private printing and publishing in England when they decided to become part of it. The concluding chapter of this book draws together observations made in the preceding ones on the dual nature of the books and considers the fruits of the Woolfs' labor at the Hogarth Press as a personal statement.

1

The Press in the Lives of the Woolfs

When the Woolfs founded the Hogarth Press in 1917, they were in their late thirties. Their marriage had been plagued in its first years by financial insecurity, severe illness and the ever-present, terrifying war of 1914-18. They had been living on the outskirts of London, in Richmond, Surrey, to distance themselves from the hurly-burly of London. Its social world was too enticing. So were the entanglements of the personal and professional lives of their friends and relatives. All the excitement fascinated but exhausted Virginia. The move to Richmond was precipitated by attacks of mental illness which she suffered intermittently from 1913 until the end of 1915. Leonard's first offer to buy a printing press for Virginia's birthday in January 1915 was deferred because of her recurring illness and his anxiety over being drafted, which was not resolved until May 1916. For the next two years, the Woolfs were preoccupied with the delicate business of putting their lives back together. By the end of 1916, both of them were leading "pretty regular" lives, working "strenuously" weekdays and taking short breaks in the country on the weekends.[1] Leonard was writing *Empire and Commerce in Africa* and making regular contributions to the *New Statesman*. He was also beginning his lifelong involvement with various committees in the Labour Party. Virginia was working again on *Night and Day* and writing short pieces of fiction as well as reviewing regularly for the *Times Literary Supplement*. She was the sort of writer who was always perfecting her craft, even in restful moments. If she was not writing, typing drafts or revising, she was thinking through passages, creating new expressions. Unfortunately, she coupled this concentrated desire to write with an obsessive fear of the publisher's reader. Leonard suggested printing as a recreation sufficiently absorbing to divert her, at least on a conscious level, from the intensity of her creative drive. It would also, he hoped, minimize her difficulty with the editor.

The creative expression of ideas was deeply ingrained in the characters of both Woolfs. They had begun communicating their ideas at the tender ages of eight and nine, when they independently established journals to circulate among their families. The *Leonard Paper* is just a memory now but the *Hyde Park Gate News*, founded by Virginia with her sister Vanessa and brother Thoby, ran weekly for several years. There is evidence too that the Woolfs considered founding a journal early in their marriage but lacked financial backing and were over-burdened with other obligations.

By March 1917, the Woolfs were no strangers to the demands of publishers and the many demands of being published. They had not only their own considerable experience as working writers but also that of Virginia's father, Sir Leslie Stephen. Stephen had known most of the literary men of the nineteenth century. The tales are numerous of Victorian publishers who controlled the lives and creative work of their authors. Stephen himself was a slave to the mammoth publication the *National Biography* for which he was editor and author. Perhaps Virginia's fears of criticism stemmed from knowledge of her father's anguish over this project. It is likely too that Stephen's editorial role at the *Cornhill Magazine* was an incentive to the Woolfs to become their own publishers. Leonard makes very clear throughout his autobiographies that publishing rather than printing was the primary reason for continuing the Press each time they were ready to give it up, even if he does not acknowledge this as the main reason for beginning it.[2]

There was a fair sense of adventure in these two people. They were determined to find a means for fulfilling their individual creative needs without the restraints and confines of the commercial publishing world. It is ironic that they were foiled in their initial pursuit of printing by the labor regulations governing trades which made no allowances for the amateur. Since neither was entering the printer's trade, they could not find a way to become schooled in the craft within the system. In the end, they gave up trying, bought a press and taught themselves from a 16-page pamphlet.

The Woolfs immediately named their venture the Hogarth Press, taking its name from their house in Richmond, whose history Leonard tells in *Beginning Again*, describing the influence houses had had on their lives.[3] Both Woolfs were greatly impressed by places where they had lived as adults and as children. So while it might have been merely convenient to name their new hobby after Hogarth House, the name evokes the Woolfs' real affection for the place as well. When the Press moved with the Woolfs back to London in 1924, it also moved from its humble spot in the dining room and back larder to more sophisticated surroundings suitable to its growing success: at Tavistock Square it had rooms of its own in the basement.

The first small hand press owned by the Woolfs was bought on the spur of the moment on March 23, 1917.[4] With it, they got all the paraphernalia necessary for printing: composing stick, type, cases, chases, and so on. Their press, about the size of a large typewriter, sat in the dining room which became the center of printing activities. It would print one demy-octavo page at a time, perhaps two crown octavo pages. (According to John Carter, *A BC for Book Collectors*, the demy-octavo, about the size of a biography or travel book, was smaller than the crown octavo, which was about the size of the average modern novel.) It worked by a simple platen device. A handle was brought down and the platen with paper on it was brought up against the type in its chase overhead. With this set-up, the Woolfs would have had to shift the sheet holding four pages four times, printing each page individually, if using the demy-octavo format, turning the sheet over and aligning the type to be printed with that already printed on the other side when they wished to print on both sides of the sheet. In all printing, keeping everything aligned and printing the pages in the proper sequence so that they fall in the correct order in the book when they are folded are the big problems. The Woolfs mastered the layout problems of book design quickly and by April were printing. But it is no wonder that when they were faced with their second job, Katherine Mansfield's *Prelude* with its 68 pages, Leonard decided to find a press that would print a full sheet at one time, and he bought such a press as soon as possible, in 1921. When they started out, the Woolfs had some Caslon Old Face and the little press; when they added the larger Minerva machine they also added more type. The Minerva was a great thing, operated by a treadle and too heavy for the dining-room floor, so the Press expanded into the larder.

The Woolfs got beyond the most elementary stages of their hobby but they were never very good printers. Leonard mentions that he had trouble from the start leveling the type in the chase. He never completly mastered the technique, just as he never got his inking consistent or black enough. Virginia took on the typesetting, which Leonard took no part in because a nervous condition made his hands shake constantly. As her frequent diary entries confirm, she set up the type and broke down the page after it had been printed by Leonard, then sorted the type into the cases.

As long as the handprinted products were primarily the work of the Woolfs, they were poorly inked and contained many typographical errors, showing that the Woolfs did not bother to correct set type from their proof sheets. Both joined in folding the sheets and stitching the signatures into books or pamphlets. The bindings were of special interest to the Woolfs, who took great pleasure over the years in finding colorful and unusual papers in which to wrap their printing efforts at the Press. Binding was a particular task of Virginia's, something she had done for pleasure as a young woman and continued to do until her death.

With *Prelude* the Woolfs realized immediately that not only could they not use their small machine, but they needed help to set the 68 pages in the chases which Leonard would then hand carry round to the Prompt Press, run by a shadowy man named McDermott who helped Leonard run them off.

From 1918 on, the Press was helped by a series of young men and women who not only set type and printed but did all sorts of odd jobs. Eventually, the Woolfs added permanent clerical help who also gave a hand with the Press work. From this situation grew the idea that a partner might be added to relieve the Woolfs of other responsibilities at the Press but this did not happen until later.

Though a steady stream of young people came to the Press after it got established who were employed as jacks-of-all-trades, some of whom may have had visions of a future as famous printers or publishers, none seems to have made a realistic assessment of the situation at hand, so most were vaguely disappointed in their experience with the Press.[5] Spater says there were several reasons for this, including slim wages and tightly controlled expenses:

> Further, because of his conviction that risks must be carefully limited, Leonard was not prepared to abdicate the right to select the books to be published.... Finally, he was not only a demanding task-master, but was inclined to doubt both the facts and the judgment of others, even on matters of minor importance, yielding only to the most incontrovertible evidence. Put more crudely, he was opinionated, he was stubborn, and he enjoyed argument. That he was usually right (and enjoyed being proved right) did not ease the problem of working in peace and harmony with others.[6]

There has been much speculation on the relationship between the staff at the Press and the Woolfs. Olsen feels that Virginia got on well with the men and Leonard was more inclined to sympathize with the women.[7] It was certainly a lively place as remembered by Richard Kennedy in his book *A Boy at the Hogarth Press*. Most of the young people, like Ralph Partridge and George Rylands, moved on more mature and wiser in the ways of the world, fulfilling their destinies by other, more tranquil means. John Lehmann was the exception. Though he too moved on, following the pattern of others after a similar first experience, Lehmann also came back to the Woolfs, walking, not thrown, as he says in the title of his book on the subject, after several years in editing, his true calling. It took another unsatisfactory round with Leonard and failure as a publisher on his own to prove this to him. His talents as an editor and literary critic are so obvious from a survey of his work in *New Writing* and *New Signatures* and the number of poets and writers he encouraged over the years that it can only be regretted that he wasted so much energy arguing with Leonard Woolf's ghost.

When he came to Press in 1931, Lehmann was a very young man of twenty-four. His sensitivity to the artistic expression of the turbulent years of the 1930s was already established. But his immaturity gave him a false sense of his own importance. As a friend of George Rylands, who had worked at the Press briefly in 1924, and of Virginia's nephew, Julian Bell, Lehmann was well informed on the situation at the Press. When he joined the Woolfs the first time, they were desperately seeking a way to escape the daily demands of a publishing firm which had become a big business. By this time, the Press had a list of more than 200 titles and had added 29 more in 1930 alone. Its success was due directly to its best-selling fiction authors, Virginia Woolf and Vita Sackville-West, and to the steady sales of topical subjects from the non-fiction list. This growth had strained not only the Woolfs but also the simple organization which they had originally devised for their hobby. This part-time job was intruding more frequently on time they wished to spend on other important projects and the whole situation made them very unhappy. Lehmann was seen as a person who could take over the management of the Press.

The long and short of the difficulties in the first arrangement between the Woolfs and Lehmann was that when they finally had to let go of their creation, they could not give up enough editorial responsibility (the heart of publishing) to satisfy Lehmann's desire to exercise his talents. For his part, Lehmann did not fully understand what "management" implies in a small shop, nor did he have any practical business experience to give him a hint of the routine, dull, detailed planning it requires. When he left abruptly after eighteen months, he was not much wiser nor more mature concerning this aspect of the publishing business. With his departure, the Woolfs became despondent and were paralyzed where problems of the Press were concerned. They struggled along through the 1930s until Lehmann's return in 1938. And they discontinued printing (which in any case seems to have been taken over by a more skilled hand for the last few publications) and concentrated on publishing at the Press.

The financial success of the Hogarth Press from its very beginning has been described by Leonard in his autobiographies. The break-even success of *Two Stories*, which was sold by subscription, was quickly exceeded by the heady success of *Kew Gardens* which required an immediate reprint by commercial printers. From this time on (1919) subscriptions were dropped since it was discovered that bookstores were buying most of the copies anyway, and Leonard branched out with his popular series of Russian translations. The handprinted books continued on the list of Hogarth Press publications through 1939, when *The Complete Catalogue of the Hogarth Press* was published, showing seventeen of these titles still in print.[8] These books were carried financially by the success of the Press as a publishing enterprise. Success allowed the Woolfs not only to print books they knew might never sell but also to expand with other publishing ideas subsidized by their commercial products, such as books of poetry (dreadfully slow sellers) and several ambitious pamphlet series, an expensive form to create and market through twentieth-century booksellers.

Before discussing the authors and the handprinted books, it is helpful to have a more intimate view of the Woolfs as individuals. The Press demanded certain talents and characteristics not often stressed in literary discussions. Since the intention of this book is to show the Press books and their authors through the comments of the Woolfs whenever possible, it is also only fitting that each Woolf should comment on the other.

Leonard described Virginia as a person who was in a continuing state of creativity. Once this essential characteristic is accepted, it is easier to see why she struck people as peculiar. Leonard says:

> There was something in Virginia which they found ridiculous. Some monstrous female caricature, who was accepted as ordinary by the crowd, would go into fits of laughter at the sight of Virginia. I always found it difficult to understand exactly what the cause of this laughter was. It was only partly that her dress was never quite the same as other people's. It was partly, I think, because there was something strange and disquieting, and therefore to many people ridiculous in her appearance, in the way she walked—she seemed to often be "thinking of something else," to be moving with a slightly shuffling movement along the streets in the shadow of a dream.[9]

Her conversation was no more ordinary than her appearance. It was frequently a fantastic fabrication, sometimes disarmingly direct and personal with a childlike disregard for the discomfiture of the individual towards whom it might be directed. It was an aspect of her personality which either enchanted or exasperated. However, her bubbling chatter and curiosity about life's trials endeared her to most of the young people who passed through the Press into the harsher world of adult responsibilities. She seems to have had a similar effect on children, who responded to her intense, if superficial, attention and enthusiastic participation in their make-believe world. Fantasizing is a very useful attribute if one is faced with the tedious task of setting type for hours on end or making an afternoon of packing and tying bundles of books for the mail.

It is often forgotten amid the gloomy stories of her mental illness that Virginia was a very active person for most of her life. It was a life filled with creative achievements, enlivened by various social activities and the rewarding effort of maintaining old friendships and embarking on new ones. It should also be remembered that Virginia walked miles daily, whether on the Sussex downs or in the streets of London; she also rode horses and later a bicycle. She was not only a competent cook but became noted for her jams, put up from Leonard's garden harvest. She worked needlepoint designs by Vanessa Bell and Duncan Grant. The bowling competition between the Woolfs became legendary, though as Spater comments, Virginia was outwitted by the sly Leonard time and again because he took advantage of her with the knowledge he gained from mowing the yards.[10]

It is not too difficult to believe Leonard Woolf capable of such an ungentlemanly act as taking advantage of his knowledge to defeat his wife. He has been described as the most controlled, rational and emphatic of the Cambridge men who fell under G.E. Moore's influence at the turn of the century. His life was a romantic quest for truth and beauty in objects and relationships, which he pursued with near fanatic intensity, searching for perfection. Leonard's writings and comments from colleagues and friends show him to have been compassionate and humane in the broad, impersonal sense of these words, but in a more earthly way, he balanced these virtues by being intolerant of stupidity or human weakness; he was also stubborn about procedure and arrogant on principle. One of his most wonderful arrogant displays is a passage in *Sowing* in which he harangues God for designing

> the stupid wastefulness of a system which requires that human beings with great labour and pain should spend years in acquiring knowledge, experience and skill, and then just when at last they might use all this in the service of mankind and for their own happiness, they lose their teeth and their hair and their wits and are hurriedly bundled, together with all that they have learnt, into the grave and nothingness.[11]

It is this mocking humor and dry, unexpected wit which save Leonard from being a bore. Virginia once said somewhere that what she enjoyed most about being married to Leonard was never knowing what he would say when he entered a room

In general, Virginia agreed with Leonard in most of the major decisions of their life together; in any case, she did not argue with him in public. The diaries reveal a steady increase of criticism of his intransigent ways. A section from *A Writer's Diary*, published by Leonard in 1953, contains a vivid picture of the relationship established between Leonard and Virginia which more recent portraits have not improved upon:

> Leonard gave me a very severe lecture on the first half [of her biography of Roger Fry]. We walked in the meadows. It was like being pecked by a very hard strong beak. The more he pecked the deeper, as always happens. At last he was almost angry that I'd chosen "what seems to me the wrong method. It's merely analysis, not history. Austere repression. In fact dull to the outsider. All those dead quotations." His theme was that you can't treat a life like that; must be seen from the writer's angle, unless the liver is himself a seer, which R. wasn't. It was a curious example of L. at his most rational and impersonal: rather impressive yet so definite, so emphatic that I felt convinced: I mean of failure: save for one odd gleam, that he was himself on the wrong tack, and persisting for some deep reason—dissympathy with R.? Lack of interest in personality? Lord knows. I note this plaited strand in my mind; and even while we walked the beak struck deeper, deeper, had this completely detached interest in L's character.[12]

After meeting the Woolfs, the socialist writer and reformer Beatrice Webb (herself in dynamic partnership with her husband Sidney Webb) gave as her considered opinion that the Woolfs were an "exceptionally gifted pair."[13] The contribution of the Hogarth Press to twentieth-century literature is one fruit of the Woolfs' combined gifts.

2

Books by the Woolfs

The first publication of the Hogarth Press, as it proudly says on the title page, is *Two Stories*. Since it was the Woolfs' first effort, this book should be seen as a product of two enthusiastic amateur printers who had mastered the rudiments of printing and binding with remarkable speed.

> *Two Stories*. Written and printed by Virginia and L.S. Woolf. 31 pages, uncut. On the title page is: "Publication no. 1." The text is illustrated with four woodcuts, unsigned and unrecognized by Carrington, two each for Leonard's *Three Jews* and Virginia's *The Mark on the Wall*. There is a table of contents. The covers vary; some have paper-backed cloth printed in red and white with an overall design and others are wrapped in plain yellow papers. The title, publisher and place of publication are printed on the cover in black in decorative type beneath the title. The cover is sewn through the pages and cover with string looping over the outside of the pamphlet. Size: 8-7/8 x 5-5/8. Hogarth Press, Richmond, 1917.

The Woolfs were so excited about publishing something that *Two Stories* was being printed before Virginia had even written her contribution. The whole experience of book production fascinated the Woolfs:

> We have just started printing Leonard's story; I haven't produced mine yet, but there's nothing in writing compared with printing.... We've got about 60 orders already which shows a trusting spirit.... (Letter to Vanessa Bell, 22 May 1917)

The realization of *Two Stories* incorporates several elements of book design which the Woolfs continued to favor in their succeeding productions, and it also has some features which were dropped from subsequent handprinted books. One of the most obvious characteristics is their use of capital letters on the cover and the title page for author, title, publisher and place of publication. This format is often used for one and sometimes, as here, for both components. A generous use of space in margins and between lines is typical. The Woolfs favored a white page rather than the black page of dark ink, close lines and closely spaced type popularized by William Morris. The Woolfs' use of space becomes a practical advantage when the reader is faced with poor inking and gray type, less admirable qualities also typical of Hogarth Press books printed by the Woolfs. *Two Stories* is sewn but the Woolfs experimented with gluing and stapling as well, often combining these methods with disastrous results by creating a very tight back which broke along the spine when the book was opened. They finally settled on a combination of gluing and sewing which worked well, though sometimes they slopped the glue or glued the pages together or ignored the use of endpapers to help support the body of the book and the whole thing fell apart anyway.

Two Stories began not only the tradition of colorful paper covers for Hogarth Press books but also that of having covers made of different materials within one print run. The reasons for this habit are not actually known but it is possible that the Woolfs simply used what was handy and bought more as they went along. Virginia makes reference from time to time to buying papers for a specific edition, though she does not seem concerned if the edition was not, finally, uniform. Perhaps they did only use what was left around but one wonders if the Woolfs' approach could really have been this haphazard. On the other hand, it happened so frequently that they could hardly have been seriously bothered by it. Maybe in the early days they could not calculate their needs accurately, since later they did consistently cover a print run in one material. It is usually mentioned by those who worked with Leonard that he was a waste-not-want-not fellow, even to the extent of reusing envelopes and providing proof sheets as toilet paper.[1] It is not likely that he would have perceived it as an eccentricity to use several kinds of paper within one edition.

There is a general tendency in the early books toward sloppiness in printing, with messy corrections littered through the text in ink or with cancel slips pasted in the back or front, all of which certainly indicates a lack of care or concern for the books' neat and tidy appearance. Oddly enough, though both were avid readers, neither of the Woolfs seems to have been affected by what for most people would have been an offensive barrier to enjoying the contents of their books. The later books are better planned and show less of this sloppiness and, on the whole, tend toward a different aesthetic. These middle and late books have a more uniform appearance and show every sign of fine attention to detail before ink was put to paper. They reflect a care for layout and design including paper selection and binding elements which is, particularly in the last books, reminiscent of Morris and the Arts and Crafts Movement. The effect actually gives them a more conventional appearance.

The title page note and inclusion of a table of contents for *Two Stories* reveal the Woolfs' ambivalence concerning the exact form future Hogarth Press publications would take. The "magazine" style may originate from their initial interest in founding a periodical, but although it would seem to begin one, *Two Stories* is not part of a series. However, this is a publishing idea which the Woolfs later took up with great success on the commercial side of the Press. The only handprinted pamphlet from a series seems to have been a fluke and the reason is now lost as to why the Woolfs printed Theodora Bosanquet's *Henry James at Work*. In the beginning, the Woolfs thought they would limit themselves to the short pamphlets they could manage with their small hand press. But their thinking shifted when they received the manuscript of *Prelude* from Katherine Mansfield, which they badly wanted as their second publication although it was too long to be accommodated on their machine.

In a sense, since Virginia had not written *The Mark on the Wall* when they began to print Leonard's story, she was "asked" to write something for the Press and this, too, turned out to be characteristic of what the Woolfs published. They often asked authors for material especially for the Press and often got something which had not been previously published. A variation of this pattern was the publication of verse which had appeared in periodicals before being collected for the first time by the Press. Such a publication can be an important event for unknown authors trying to reach a public and giving them this opportunity was a prime motive for the Woolfs.

A final element of *Two Stories* which the Woolfs felt strongly about at the beginning of the Press but which had less importance later is illustration or the touch of an artist. For their first production, the Woolfs asked their friend Dora Carrington, Lytton Strachey's companion, to provide four woodcuts. Carrington, never called Dora, trained at the Slade School of Art under Steer and Tonks and won several scholarships and prizes. She knew Mark Gertler and other younger artists active in London before the First World War as well as the "bright young things" who gathered at Lady Ottoline Morrell's house parties—Lady Dorothy Brett, Katherine Mansfield and Barbara Hiles Begenal, to name but a few of the women. When she gave up her career in art to manage Strachey's domestic life, Carrington entered the circle of the Woolfs' intimate friends, though she would have already known Vanessa Bell and Duncan Grant because of their affiliation with the art world. Leonard was particularly fond of Carrington, whom he described as a Chinese box puzzle, and asked her to illustrate his other handprinted book too.[2] It was through Strachey and Carrington that the Woolfs got to know Ralph Partridge and to take him on as their first "young man" at the Press in the early 1920s.

The Woolfs do not seem to have worried much about the technical problems involved in printing Carrington's blocks for *Two Stories*:

We like the wood cuts immensely. It was very good of you to bring them yourself—we have printed them off and they make the book more interesting than it would have been without. The ones I like best are the servant girl and the plates and the snail. Our difficulty was that the margins would mark; we bought a chisel, and chopped away, I am afraid rather spoiling one edge.... We see that we must make a practice of always having pictures. (Letter to Dora Carrington, 13 July 1917)

There is not much consideration expressed here for the artist's feelings toward her creation so vigorously attacked by the Woolfs with their chisel. The printing was still terrible, with gray blotches and no life. The designs show a wondrous incongruity of style and proportion but this does not seem to have bothered the Woolfs' aesthetic sensibilities either. It is rather sad that they gave their artists so little credit. It is a small but important detail of publishing which would probably have been much appreciated. In Carrington's case, it may have been her preference to remain anonymous. She does not discuss the woodcuts for either book she worked on for Leonard at any length in her published writings, and most of the work illustrated in a biography by her brother show that she rarely signed anything.[3] The Woolfs' casual attitude toward printing illustrations and their failure to give recognition to Carrington were not taken lightly by Vanessa Bell when she made woodcuts for Virginia's *Kew Gardens*. In the end, the Woolfs were overcome by the difficulties of dealing with artists and printing their work and turned their attention to printing the text better. Only nine of the thirty-four handprinted books are illustrated by an artist; the number could have been ten but the Woolfs rejected the illustrations for *Prelude* after just a few were printed.

Though the Press published nearly a dozen titles by Leonard, it only handprinted one other volume of fiction by him. His two novels were published before the Press was founded.

Stories of the East. By Leonard Woolf. 55 pages, cut. The cover is a buff, thick paper wrapper with a front design printed in red by Carrington, unsigned and unrecognized. It is both glued and stapled. The verso of the last printed page has advertisements for current Hogarth Press publications. There are no endpapers. Size: 8 x 4-7/8. Printed and published by Leonard and Virginia Woolf at the Hogarth Press, Hogarth House, Richmond, 1921.

This is a good example of the early handprinted books.

We are well launched upon the work of the Press ... We are bringing out Three Stories by L.... (*Diary*, 18 October 1920)

Leonard's book will be printed by the end of the week perhaps. (*Diary*, 21 February 1921)

The Daily mail says that Leonard has written one of the greatest stories of the world. In consequence we are flooded with orders.... (Letter to Vanessa Bell, 13 May 1921)

The printing of the front cover gave the Woolfs some difficulty, mainly because the block was too large for the press and the thick paper too soft. The text is nicely arranged, though typically too lightly inked and unevenly printed. Several copies I examined were unopened, which leads to the question, in spite of the favorable review, of who bought it and why.

Five books were printed by the Woolfs before they printed Virginia's first individual volume yet its printing is unbelievably poor and the states are a bibliographic nightmare.

Kew Gardens. By Virginia Woolf. 16 pages, uncut. The label notes "with woodcuts by Vanessa Bell." There are two woodcuts, one in the front and one in the back of the book, but they exist in three states; some are printed on the page, others on a separate paper and pasted onto the page, and still others are printed on a separate page and pasted over those printed on the text page. The cover is a heavy black paper wrapper, handcolored with flat paint in blue, brown and orange (probably by Roger Fry); it is both glued and sewn. The label is white, printed in black with a note in italics, upper and lower case, with the artist's name in caps. Size varies from 9 x 5-1/8 to 9-3/8 x 5-7/8. Hogarth Press, Richmond, 1919. There is a colophon on the last page pasted over a printed note: "L. and V. Woolf" over "Leonard and Virginia at the Hogarth Press, Richmond."

The variations in size and the state of the woodcuts are not the only inconsistencies in this edition. The publisher's statement on the title page is augmented by a colophon printed below the text on the last page. The Woolfs do not seem to have known if the book should have been for private distribution, for those on a first-name basis only perhaps, or for the general reading public. However, their major problem was printing the woodcuts correctly.

The printing of *Kew Gardens* caused more entries in Virginia's letters and diaries than any other book handprinted by the Woolfs. Most of the serious conversations between Virginia and Vanessa took place in person but they were all painful for Virginia:

Nessa and I quarrelled as nearly as we ever do quarrel now over the get up of Kew Gardens, both type and woodcuts; and she firmly refused to illustrate any more stories of mine under those circumstances & went so far as to doubt the value of The Hogarth Press altogether.... An ordinary printer would do better in her opinion. This both stung and chilled me. (*Diary*, June 1919)

Vanessa Bell was educated at home, as was Virginia, and at the Royal Academy under Sargent. She married her brother's Cambridge friend, Clive Bell, who was also a classmate of Leonard's. They settled in the Bloomsbury section of London, where she founded the Friday Club to exhibit the work of anti-establishment artists. Bell was co-director with Roger Fry and Duncan Grant of the Omega Workshops, which ran from 1913 to 1919. She and Grant continued an active interest in interior design and the decorative arts after the Workshops closed. Bell made no secret of her opinion of Leonard's taste and skills in printing, so any project which involved both of them was a great deal of trouble. However, contrary to her threat, she continued to design all the covers for Virginia's books even after her death, when Leonard brought out her work posthumously.

The anguish surrounding *Kew Gardens* was not just personal for Virginia but also creative, since she was exploring a new kind of realism in this story and its publication through the Press was part of her dream of freedom to write and print what she herself had done. There was some delay between the publication and reception of this book which only increased her tension. But the episode ended gloriously with a glowing review in the *Times Literary Supplement*, and the orders came pouring in.

The last book of Virginia's to be handprinted was also one of the last books printed by the Woolfs. It is one of the showpieces in the private press tradition and thus quite unlike the other books discussed so far.

> *On Being Ill*. By Virginia Woolf. 35 pages, cut. Illustrated with a tailpiece, unsigned, by Vanessa Bell; there is a half title page before the limited edition notice. The cover is pale blue-green cloth with a vellum spine, printed in gilt; the dust cover is white, printed in gray, black and yellow with a design, unsigned, by Vanessa Bell. The endpapers are marbled in blues and grays. The paper for the text is very fine with a distinctive watermark. Size: 8 x 5 - 1/8. Printed and published by Leonard & Virginia Woolf at the Hogarth Press, 1930.

What distinguished *On Being Ill* and the books which follow it is a feel and sensitivity which are immediately discernible to sight and touch. The printed dust jacket; the use of gilt, which is difficult to handle and adds its own sense of quality; the vellum spine; fine papers; black ink: all these elements give a sense of pretension and preciousness which are out of character for the Woolfs and contrary to their original aesthetic concepts. *On Being Ill* looks as if it had been designed as a smart commercial publication or at least as an attempt to emulate such a style by hand. It is finely printed, with good ink color, good arrangement, well bound and with a distinctive if commercially slick cover, probably printed by offset. Though it might be argued that this book reflected the newly found wealth and social position which came to Virginia after her bestselling decade of the 1920s, the concept and execution seem rather to indicate the interests and influences of the younger men and women who had come to the Press with hopes of learning the fine art of printing, inspired by the heroic feats of contemporaries at the Golden Cockerel Press or Basil Blackwell at the Shakespeare Head Press, their standards derived from the past, from the Arts and Craft Movement and William Morris at the Kelmscott Press.

3

Books by Friends

It is, as a rule, a matter of speculation as to why the Woolfs printed and published any given piece, but the books which came from people who were friends really need only friendship as a reason for their existence in the Hogarth Press list. For some authors, such as T.S. Eliot, publication was certainly rooted in the Woolfs' desire to support a talent they felt deserved a wider audience and to give the author the added self-esteem which comes from having a work in print. In other cases, as with Fredegond Shove and Clive Bell, the reasons for printing were more personal, "in the family," a true gesture of affection. The publication of Cecil Woolf's *Poems* was so private an expression of grief that it is painful even today to view the Woolfs' small memorial to him.

The information concerning the publication of the books under consideration in this chapter gives a rather clear view of the relationship between the Woolfs and their authors. Ever present among these sketches is the image of Cambridge University in the background with frequent glimpses of the "Apostles" (as members of the Cambridge Conversazione Society were called), who tie so many of these people to the Woolfs. Either directly or indirectly, both institutions brought to their attention many individuals spanning the two generations from Roger Fry to George Rylands. It is also important to mention once again two friends who appear throughout this study but were never published by the Woolfs: Lady Ottoline Morrell and Lytton Strachey.

Strachey was Leonard's closest friend at Cambridge and kept him informed on the activities of their mutual acquaintances while he was in Ceylon between 1904 and 1911. Strachey was also an old family friend of the Stephens and was actually engaged to Virginia for a few hours before both had second thoughts about the arrangement. Strachey was well established as a literary figure in London before the Press was founded, and it was through this fame that he entered the social and literary salons where he collected the latest news on the up-and-coming young talent of his day, which he then relayed to the Woolfs over tea or during weekends in the country.

Lady Ottoline Morrell was a generous patron of the arts during the first decades of the twentieth century and an early subscriber to the Hogarth Press. Her house parties in London and at her country home, Garsington, were a great source of gossip and amusement to many of the Woolfs' friends, particularly Clive Bell and Lytton Strachey. Lady Ottoline's place in the development of British literature during this period has not been fully appreciated, and there is reason to assign her an important role in her relationship to several of the people discussed here.

The Woolfs' connection to Clive Bell had been friendly but they were less closely involved with him by the time the Press was operating. Bell was an English critic of art and literature, the only member of the Bloomsbury Group to unite an interest in a sporting, country life with the urbane tastes of the cosmopolitan. Though he was at Kings when Leonard was at Trinity, he was never an Apostle. By 1917, his marriage to Vanessa was mere formality. For the Woolfs, Bell was always a lively, if argumentative, conversationalist but a light thinker who never reached his potential, someone who enjoyed the good life but was a trifle loud and hearty for the fun-loving but more restrained Woolfs. The commercial side of the Press published Bell's study of Marcel Proust but the Woolfs handprinted two books for him.

> *Poems.* By Clive Bell. 29 pages, uncut. There is a preface. The cover is a stiff, buff paper wrapper designed but unsigned by Duncan Grant with a red clover pattern on the front only, arranged around a field with title, author and publisher printed in red on the wrapper. Size: 8 x 5-1/4. Printed & published by Leonard and Virginia Woolf at the Hogarth Press, Richmond, Surrey, 1921.

This is a slight but attractive volume, well designed with a charming cover, generous margins, nicely spaced typed, well printed. I was able to see only one copy and it was unopened, making it impossible to see the title page, always a significant aspect of the Woolfs' books. Bell states in the preface that the seventeen poems have been published elsewhere and lists the *Nation*, the *New Statesman*, the *Cambridge Magazine*, and a previous volume of poems, *Ad Familiars*. Though Bell says here that he accepted "with joy an offer by the Hogarth Press to publish a complete edition of my poems," Virginia gives a different version in her diary (1 March 1921): "Now Clive proposes we should bring out his private poems."

> *The Legend of Monte Della Sibilla or Le Paradis de la Reine Sibille.* By Clive Bell. 25 pages, uncut. Dedicated to Polly Flinders. It is illustrated with a frontispiece and headpiece as well as a cover by Vanessa Bell, whose initials are incorporated into her design, and Duncan Grant,

whose contribution is unsigned. The white dust jacket is printed with the title, author, price and the note "With decorations and cover designed by Duncan Grant and Vanessa Bell" above the publication statement. The cover is white paperboard printed in black; the dust jacket is also black on white; the book is sewn and glued. Size: 10-1/4 x 7. Printed and published by Leonard and Virginia Woolf at the Hogarth Press, Hogarth House, Richmond, 1923.

This is one of the larger format books produced by the Woolfs and it is very nicely designed, showing the close attention which the artists gave to its production. It has generous margins, fairly dark type, and is rather consistently well printed. The text has several complex passages with italics, Greek, Italian and English. All the copies of this narrative poem which I saw were either partially or totally unopened, showing here, as in his collected poems, that Clive Bell may have been bought but was not read. By this time, most of the Hogarth Press books were being bought by booksellers. Virginia mentions the printing of this book twice in her writings. She forgot the drawings while visiting Charleston, the Bells' country home, and sent a postcard to Clive asking for them; earlier in November, she notes in her diary: "But I must descend to the basement and see whats doing with Clive's cover, which Leonard does for 8 hours daily" (*Diary*, 3 November 1923).[1] She is probably talking about the dust jacket, which carries a note on the decorations and artists which looks suspiciously like an afterthought. This book is not mentioned in any of the various books on Bell or the artists.

Duncan Grant had by this time established an artistic and emotional partnership with Vanessa Bell. Some critics say their work is indistinguishable, but Grant is the finer designer, although the two artists share a free-flowing line and similar subject matter. Grant attended St. Paul's School in London, as did Leonard several years before him, and the Westminster School of Art. After study in Italy and Paris at the Atelier de la Palette, he established himself in London before the First World War and was quickly assimilated into the group of friends accumulated by his cousin, Lytton Strachey. Grant was a member of Vanessa Bell's Friday Club and co-director with her and Fry of the Omega Workshops. He is perhaps best known today as part of the English Post-Impressionist movement and as a proponent of the decorative arts style which grew out of it, exemplified of course by products from the Workshops. Clive Bell's *The Legend of Monte Della Sibilla* was a tribute from the Press to the combined skills of Duncan Grant and Vanessa Bell in the decorative arts as well as a lovely presentation volume for Bell himself to distribute; unfortunately, the identity of the dedicatee, Polly Flinders, has not been established.

Leonard probably met T.S. Eliot before Virginia at one of Lady

Ottoline's parties, or they may have been introduced by Strachey. However, Eliot was also assistant editor of the *Egoist* from 1917 until its demise in 1919 (after Clive Bell, among others, refused to take over its funding) so opportunities for the Woolfs to meet Eliot were numerous. Leonard had an inscribed copy of Eliot's *Prufrock and Other Observations* which he recalled reading shortly after it was published in 1917. The most important meeting between Eliot and the Woolfs must have been in November of 1918 when Virginia invited Eliot to tea and asked him to bring some of his poems. The Woolfs came to regard Eliot as one of their best friends. Publishing his poems was one of the highlights of this friendship and of the Woolfs' printing and publishing experience. It was not only that they were still enjoying the pleasures of their hobby, though this is clear from Virginia's letters of the time. The poems as they materialized, letters becoming words, forming line after line on the page, entranced the Woolfs as the lines became readable on the printed page. Leonard tries to explain this feeling in *Beginning Again*, describing setting *Poems*:

> as an amateur printer and also the publisher of what I was printing, I found it impossible not to attend to the sense and usually after setting a line and then seeing it appear again as I took it off the machine, I got terribly irritated by it. But I never tired and still do not tire of those lines which were a new note in poetry . . . (and sounded with even greater depth and volume in the next work of his which we published, the poem which had greatest influence upon English poetry, indeed upon English literature, than any other in the 20th century *The Waste Land*.)[2]

Poems is a typical pamphlet in the style and manner of execution exhibited by the best books from the early Press.

> *Poems*. By T.S. Eliot. 13 pages, uncut. The cover and label vary within the print run. Some books were wrapped with the printed cloth-backed paper used for *Two Stories* in 1917 and others were wrapped with a blue and black marbled paper later used for E.M. Forster's *The Story of the Siren* of 1920. The labels were printed in either red or black on white stock (the only example seen where the label changed within the edition). Size: 9-1/4 x 6-1/8. Printed & published by L. and V. Woolf at the Hogarth Press, Hogarth House, Richmond, 1919.

The book is well printed; the ink is fairly black and consistent. The printers had neatly managed a text demanding English, French and Greek with frequent italics as well. This particular book shows the Woolfs' search for a comfortable publication statement with the use of "L. and V. Woolf," which eventually became an almost standard "Leonard and Virginia Woolf." But the use or non-use of the ampersand, a favorite stylistic convention in Virginia's personal writing, was never settled and for years came and went in the publication statement of the handprinted books. Virginia writes of this volume that it was "our best work so far by a long way, owing to the quality of the ink."[3]

The Waste Land had already been published in the *Criterion*, founded by Eliot, in its October 1922 issue and in America by Dial Press at the same time. But for Eliot and the English public, it was a special event when the Woolfs finally brought out their edition in 1923. Virginia remarked in her diary:

> Eliot dined last Sunday & read his poem. He sang it & chanted it, rhymed it. It has great beauty & force of phrase: symmetry; & intensity. What connects it together I'm not so sure. But he read till he had to rush—letters to write about the London Magazine—& discussion thus was curtailed. One was left, however, with some strong emotion. The Waste Land it is called; & Mary Hutch, who has heard it more quietly, interprets it to be Tom's auto-biography—a melancholy one. (*Diary*, 23 June 1922)

The Waste Land. By T.S. Eliot. 35 pages, uncut. There is a half-title before the title page, and an advertisement on the recto of the back free endpaper. The cover is blue marbled paper-covered boards with signatures both glued and sewn. The label exists in several states, each a different size: some are boxed with asterisks; others have a single rule above and one below the title; others have no rules. Size: 9 x 5-1/2. Printed and published by Leonard and Virginia Woolf at the Hogarth Press, Hogarth House, Paradise Road, Richmond, Surrey, 1923.

There are hand-corrected errors in all the copies I reviewed, some done by Eliot and others possibly by Virginia, but considering the text requirements, the whole thing is printed amazingly well. There are passages in English, Greek, Latin, Italian, French and German as well as several pages of footnotes with complicated punctuation and much use of italics for sources cited. It is small wonder that Virginia comments at one point, "we had a desperate afternoon printing,"[4] and at another:

> we have finished Tom, much to our relief. He will be published this August by Marjorie (Joad) although we have worked at full speed since May . . . that is I'm persuaded the root & source & origin of all health & happiness, provided of course that one rides work as a man rides a great horse, in a spirited independent way; not a drudge but a man with spurs in his heels. (*Diary*, 28 July 1923)

As usual, the text of *The Waste Land* is not black enough for comfortable reading and there are some light places from uneven inking. Why the Woolfs made a habit of printing several label styles for an edition is a mystery when they knew by the time the labels were needed how many books were in the run.

The Woolfs' casual indifference toward bibliographic consistency is well established by now in this study. There was no doubt in the Woolfs' minds that this book would sell, so the publication statement includes the full address and, though the Woolfs may have considered *The Waste Land* a work of genius, they had no qualms about attaching a list of previous Hogarth titles to the endpaper, a practice begun in 1920 with E.M. Forster's *Song of the Siren*. At least in this instance, they were considerate enough of the text not to place the advertisements opposite a printed page or on the verso of the last text page. Publishing *The Waste Land* increased the Woolfs' prestige and that of the Press enormously. It also encouraged Eliot, who was still working at Lloyd's Bank, to keep writing.

Leonard and E.M. Forster were old friends from Cambridge days, though they had been at different colleges and in slightly different years; both men were Apostles and had many friends in common. When Leonard returned from the Civil Service in Ceylon, the friendship was resumed though one lived mainly in London and the other near Cambridge. Unlike Eliot, who went from the Hogarth Press to Faber and Faber when he began working there as an editor, Forster was already an established author when the Woolfs began looking for writers for the Press. The Woolfs handprinted two books for Forster but then published only two other pieces, *Anonymity, an Enquiry* for the Hogarth Essay Series and *A Letter to Madame Blanchard* for the Hogarth Letter Series. Forster, like Strachey, was committed to commercial publishers who could offer more to the working writer than the meager "percent after cost" arrangements of the Woolfs and the scarcely more than word-of-mouth advertisement campaigns mounted by Leonard to announce his publications, at least until circulars and newspaper ads were added for publicity after the subscription system was abandoned and booksellers became the chief customers for Hogarth books.

> *The Story of the Siren.* By E.M. Forster. 14 pages, uncut. The title page has an ornamental type or fleuron used as a decorative device. The last page facing the text lists previous Hogarth Press publications. The cover is a paper wrapper, both glued and stapled. The covers and labels vary: some covers I saw were green, gray and orange marbled paper; some were in the blue material used for Eliot's *Poems*, printed in 1919; others were the diamond-patterned paper used for Hope Mirrless' *Paris*, printed the same year as this story but using the pattern vertically rather than horizontally as *Story* does. The labels appear in at least three sizes and states: white card stock edged in gold printed in black within a triple frame of gold with *The Story of the* / *Siren* / E.M. Forster; the same card but reading *The Story* / *of the Siren* / E.M. Forster; and plain white stock printed in black reading *The Story of the Siren* / E.M. Forster. Size: 9-

1/2 x 5-3/4. Printed by Leonard & Virginia Woolf at the Hogarth Press, Paradise Road, Richmond, 1920.

This small pamphlet with all its variations is in general like all the early books with a few less common elements. The printing of the story was a straightforward matter which the Woolfs handled with their usual blend of uneven inking and generous spacing. This is the first time an ornament type was used since the cover of *Two Stories*, but it is used on and off throughout the handprinted books. With this volume, the Woolfs started to place advertisements in their publications. It seems oddly out of place to modern readers but has a long tradition in publishing, particularly before the age of best-sellers and massive advertisement programs. As with other early books, this one is folded and the body stapled and then glued to the cover wrapper with occasional sloppy results. The books in the run vary as much as those in any other produced by the Woolfs with the possible exception of Fredegond Shove's *Daybreak* and it is possible that not all the versions have yet been accounted for. Virginia comments to Lady Ottoline:

> I must now get my scissors and paste and start again upon the Siren. Did you like her? I can't judge any of our productions when I've done with them; in fact they cease to be literature in an early stage of the process. (Letter to Lady Ottoline Morrell, 18 July 1920)

This passage shows not only a busy Virginia, pitching in to get the order out, but also the dribble style of their small operation: a few orders off right away to a supporter such as Lady Ottoline and then a few more with each mail, or so they hoped. Earlier, Virginia had noted in her diary:

> We work like navvies at binding Morgan & have no time for frivolity. . . . it looks as though Morgan might boom, though I don't as a critic, see altogether what the reason is. (*Diary*, 6 July 1920)

According to Forster's biographer, P.N. Furbank, this story was given to the Woolfs when they asked for something for the Press. Forster wrote it to be published in a magazine but none would take it.[5]

Pharos and Pharillon. By E.M. Forster. 80 pages, uncut. Advertisement for three of the author's other books appears opposite the title page; the dedication is in Greek; acknowledgements thank the *Nation* and the *Athenaeum* for five chapters and C.P. Cavafy for permission to print his poems and George Valassopoulo for translating them. The last page lists previously published books by the Press. The cover is made of boards covered with a white paper shot with shades of blue. It appears in two states, with the design horizontal or vertical. The white label appears on a blue cloth spine with rules at the top and bottom and a small decorative type (different from that used on the title page of *Story*) separating the title from the author. Size varies: 8-1/2 x 5-1/2 to 8-3/4 x 5-5/8. Printed and published by Leonard and Virginia Woolf at the Hogarth Press, Paradise Road, Richmond, Surrey, 1923.

It is obvious that the Woolfs had mastered their binding problems, and they managed a substantial-feeling book in *Pharos and Pharillon*. It looks almost commercial, in fact, which may have been their intent since the edition ran to 900 copies, several times more than the average edition for one of their handprinted books. In general it is well printed, the ink is fairly black, and the spacing, which varies widely throughout the text, is usually generous and complementary to the material. The text includes both narrative passages and quotes rendered in lower point type. It also has a section of poetry by Constantine Cavafy, a Greek poet introduced to English readers by Forster but more familiar now from quotations in Lawrence Durrell's *The Alexandria Quartet*. Such diversity in the text would challenge any designer or typesetter but by this time the Woolfs had published several demanding texts and this one is well done. Forster was working on a guide to Alexandria when he was overcome by depression at the death of a young man with whom he had been in love during his visit to Egypt. He decided to write his impressions of the city, taking his title from the names of its two ancient lighthouses. The dedication is a circumspect reference to the young man. As expected, this book sold very well and was reprinted commercially several times.

Roger Fry was an engaging and entertaining companion who made many visits to Cambridge and attended Apostle meetings for years after he left the university. He became very friendly with younger members such as Woolf, Forster and Strachey. Fry's friendship with Vanessa Bell and the establishment of the Omega Workshops, which also produced books, just at the time when Leonard and Virginia were thinking of going into publishing, certainly added new dimensions to the Woolfs' vague plans. By the time they considered doing Fry's *Twelve Original Woodcuts* for the Press, they had printed and published eleven books, several with decorations more or less successfully printed around the text, including *Two Stories, Prelude, Paris, Kew Gardens*, and *Stories of the East*. Fry's book, a courageous undertaking considering their past experiences with artists, is unique in that it has no text, and aside from the title page and a list of titles for the woodcuts, which was dropped in the second and third impressions, it consists entirely of woodcuts. There is, however, a list of Hogarth Press publications in the back, another example no doubt of Leonard taking advantage of a good seller at the expense of aesthetic considerations.

Twelve Original Woodcuts. By Roger Fry. Unpaginated with 12 plates, cut. The cover of the first impression has a marbled paper wrapper made by Fry, stitched and glued with a white label printed in black with a decorative band at the top and bottom. Size: 9 x 6-1/2. Printed and published by Leonard and Virginia Woolf at the Hogarth Press, Hogarth House, Richmond, 1921.

This book is far better printed than *Kew Gardens*. The Woolfs must have had help from Fry to achieve the quality of the prints in this book: "Roger again last night, scraping at his woodcuts while I sewed; the sound like that of a large pertinacious rat."[6] As with *Kew Gardens*, there are several states for this book, not because of poor printing but because it sold out so quickly. Virginia records in frantic letters to friends how the first and second editions ran out almost as fast as the Woolfs could print and stitch them until they finally ran a third impression. The second and third impressions are identical except for the note "Second Impression" or "Third Impression" on the title page: off-white wrappers with the last woodcut reproduced on the cover along with the title and artist in caps. The first impression was wrapped in marbled paper provided by Fry. The Woolfs had already begun to use Fry's marbled papers in 1919, for Eliot's *Poems*. They were used for *Kew Gardens* and *The Story of the Siren* before finally covering Fry's own handprinted volume from the Woolfs. He had his own methods of marbling or coloring papers, just as he had his own methods and techniques for throwing and decorating china or decorating furniture and weaving rugs for the Workshops. Rather than using the traditional method of suspending color on water and floating it onto the paper, Fry took discarded wallpaper (not a new idea for wrapping sewn signatures but it does suggest the phrase "stiff and brittle") which was far too heavy and poor in quality for the purpose he intended, and simply flung colors on it in random patterns, alternating large and small splashes until he had filled an area to his satisfaction. The flat paint, like poster paint today, soon dulled with dirt. Eventually the Woolfs either bought papers when they traveled or got them from Fry's daughter, Pamela Diamand, who had learned the art of marbling properly in Paris.[7]

The woodcuts themselves are beautifully printed and the book is a lovely, fresh expression of Fry's talent as a designer. Strangely enough, they are given no attention in the material which has been published about Fry or in his letters. Donald A. Laing mentions the Hogarth Press book in his bibliography on Fry but there is no comment about it.[8] Laing's list notes that this is Fry's only book devoted entirely to woodcuts. Fry did, however, illustrate a book for C.H. Ashbee, who was a fellow student at Cambridge and an energetic contributor to the Arts and Craft Movement in Great Britain. Later, Fry did illustrations for two books of poetry by R.C. Trevelyan, who was also a

Cambridge friend and shared a house with Fry for several years. Neither of these books, unfortunately, is the one printed by the Woolfs for Trevelyan, but one of them was published by the Omega Workshops.

Another book published by the Workshops has four of Fry's woodcuts in it and was originally to have been produced by the Hogarth Press. According to Richard Shone, Vanessa Bell wrote to Fry about it in August 1917: "Virginia has asked me to get together enough woodcuts to produce one of their numbers—of woodcuts only which will be fun. I have always wanted to try to do some again. Will you contribute?" This was before Vanessa tangled with the Woolfs over *Kew Gardens*. Shone goes on to say:

> Roger started work and Vanessa and Duncan did some; at the Omega, de Bergan and Edward Wolfe were also asked to contribute. By September the project was called off, Vanessa unable to have the last word aesthetically over the production and unwilling to trust Leonard's taste.[9]

She had seen what the Woolfs did with a chisel to Carrington's blocks for *Two Stories* and seen examples of their amateurish approach to printing, which must have seemed not only presumptuous but sacrilegious to a professional artist.

The Woolfs published four other works by Fry at the Hogarth Press, including his famous discussion of Paul Cézanne and a book on Castille with reproductions of Fry's sketches in a limited edition specially produced by the commercial Press.

The Woolfs seem to have met George Rylands either through the economist John Maynard Keynes or Lytton Strachey; they were together with Keynes in Dorset in September of 1923 when Rylands was approached about working for the Press. He comments:

> I had many happy hours setting up type with Virginia and helping Leonard with the hand press (or battling inkily and unsuccessfully with it on my own)—doing up parcels, selling books to travelers—meeting their friends—listening and talking about literature....[10]

Rylands, known to his friends as "Dadie," left for Kings to become a Shakespearean scholar and teacher. As his replacement Rylands brought another Cambridge man, Angus Davidson, into the Woolfs' fold to help at the Press. Rylands remained a good friend and strengthened their connections with new talent coming down from the university. They published his thesis on poetry and handprinted two collections of his poems. And when the third series of Hogarth Lectures was begun in 1951, Rylands took on the editorship.

> *Russet and Taffeta*. By George Rylands. 8 pages, cut. The title page uses open-faced Caslon type and displays the small wolf's head printer's

device designed by Vanessa Bell. It is dedicated to Virginia Woolf. The cover has a russet brown, black and gray marbled paper wrapper with a cream label printed in black within a double frame (outer line thick, inner thin). Size: 10-1/4 x 8. Printed & published by Leonard & Virginia Woolf at the Hogarth Press, 52 Tavistock Square, London, 1925.

This small booklet is a nearly perfect example of printing in the book arts tradition, with extra care taken in the spacing and printing of the title page. The title page shows for the first time in the handprinted books the open-faced type which distinguishes the middle and later productions from the earlier ones with their heavy, solid look. Here, too, is the first use of the wolf's head, which is used in different ways in later handprinted books. The text is as meticulously arranged as the title page, though it offered no particular difficulties, with only a few instances of italics and some irregular uses of punctuation. In response to Rylands' offer to dedicate this volume to her, Virginia replied in the manner which made so many adore her:

> Of course it will give me enormous pleasure to have your poems dedicated to me, and Old Woolf himself can find no objection to it. So we shall do it .... If I weren't overcome by the bashful timidity which is a mark of my nature (and one of the reasons why I am such a nice woman in spite of all you can say to the contrary) I should fling my arms around you and tell you so. Yes, it gives me enormous pleasure. (Letter to George Rylands, 20 July 1925)

The tidy endpapers of plain white hide the stitching and gluing and give this little booklet a finished but not commercial look. Its exection gives pleasure to the reader on several levels, reflecting Rylands' own pleasure in finely printed books. He once considered joining John Lehmann in beginning a private press, and whether or not his hand was actually set to this volume, it reflects his spirit and sense of taste.

Poems. By George Rylands. Unpaginated and uncut. Dedicated "to the authoress of *Dusty Answer* and the authoress of *Inigo Sandys*." The cover is a paper-covered board in light green, dark green and brown herringbone design with a white label printed in black. There is a plain tissue dust jacket. Size: 7 x 4-1/4. Printed & published by L. & V. Woolf at the Hogarth Press, London, 1931.

This is one of the very best of the late publications in an unusual format, so neat and distinguished by its fulfillment of the traditional requirements for a finely printed private press book. The title page design has taken into account the long, slender shape of the page and the publication statement too is shortened from the more familiar "Leonard and Virginia" back to an older version, "L. & V. Woolf." Most noticeable is the use of lower case where it has been usual to find all caps. This collection of twelve poems did not offer any more difficult textual problems for the typesetter than Rylands' first book, though it has passages in French and makes use of italics for emphasis. His line formation has made the inner margin a little more difficult to control and make pleasing to the eye. The two writers mentioned in the dedication are John Lehmann's sister, Rosamond Lehmann, who wrote *Dusty Answer*, and Emily Beatrix Courolles (E.B.C.) Jones, the wife of writer F.L. Lucas, who wrote *Inigo Sandys*. Since Virginia asks Rylands if he likes the look of his poems, it is plain that he took an interest in how the book was produced, but again, it is unclear whether he actually participated in its making.

The Woolfs knew Vita Sackville-West very well. They were not only the publishers of her best-selling novels but intimate friends, with interests and ties beyond the Bloomsbury Group, of which Sackville-West was not a member. The pleasures of country living and gardening were two of their shared interests. In 1930, Sackville-West and her husband Harold Nicolson bought a ruined castle in Kent which they spent the rest of their lives putting into liveable condition and surrounding with superb gardens designed for the most part by Harold and supervised to perfection by Vita. The poem *Sissinghurst* was written as a letter to Virginia in early November 1930, just after the Nicolsons had found this castle. Since the women met a few days later, the idea of a special publication honoring the find, Virginia and their friendship must have been born at that time. Leonard advertised it as a forthcoming book in the *Times* on January 9, 1931.

> *Sissinghurst*. By V. Sackville-West. Unpaginated and uncut. The cover is board, covered in brown marbled paper, printed with the publication information in brown; there are blue-green endpapers. The work is dedicated to "V.W." Size: 8-5/8 x 6-7/8. Printed by hand by Leonard & Virginia Woolf and published by the Hogarth Press, London, 1931.

This is the thirty-second book printed by the Woolfs. It is one of the most perfectly designed and executed of all the handprinted books. It appears to be printed on a half-sheet, printed and folded as a quarto with the deckled edge at the tail. The paper is crisp, the ink black and the binding careful. It shows the hand of John Lehmann, who was at the Press between 1931 and 1932. The type spacing is nicely balanced, the body of the text well placed in the generous margin of white. It is a beautiful example of a book in the private press tradition: an extravagant effort to print five pages beautifully. Virginia was pleased with the effort and the gesture of affection from Vita:

> Well, that is a nice good poem. Yes, I like it. I like its suavity and ease; and its calm; and its timelessness and shade; and its air of rings widening till they imperceptibly touch the bank. That's what I like best in your work. (Letter to V. Sackville-West, 16 November 1930)

There were at least 500 copies printed and some I saw were noted as being out of series. *Sissinghurst* was favorably reviewed in the *Manchester Guardian*. Sackville-West was well known during this period for her poetry, particularly her prize-winning *The Land*, also set in the Kent countryside, and *Sissinghurst* quickly went out of print. The Press published thirteen books for Sackville-West, including several popular travel books, her most enduring novel, *The Edwardians*, and the biography of her infamous grandmother, *Pepita*.

Fredegond Maitland Shove was Virginia's cousin and the wife of another Cambridge graduate, the economist Gerald Shove. She wrote several books of poetry, an autobiography, and a biography of Christina Rossetti which is still in print. Her main place in literature or history, however, seems to have been at the side of her husband. The Shoves were part of the contingency of conscientious objectors who took refuge at Phillip and Ottoline Morrell's farm, Garsington, during the First World War.

Fredegond is mentioned regularly in Virginia's letters and diaries, and the two shared bits of family news and gossip. Quentin Bell describes her as "a very intense and poetic young woman."[11] She belonged to that group of women which included several former Slade School students met before in this study: Lady Dorothy Brett, Dora Carrington, and Barbara Hiles Bagenal, who was the second paid employee at the Press. Its first paid employee was Fredegond's friend Alix Sargent-Florence Strachey, who worked at the Press for one hour typesetting Mansfield's *Prelude* until she quit from boredom. It is from the context of such interweaving interests and personalities that the Woolfs' desire to publish Fredegond's poetry came. The Woolfs' book, *Daybreak*, was not her first book of poems. Basil Blackwell had published *Dreams and Journeys* in 1918 as part of his "Series of Young Poets Unknown to Fame."

> *Daybreak*. By Fredegond Shove. 42 pages, uncut. The book is dedicated to "My sister Ermengard Maitland." There are advertisements for previously published books and forthcoming publications on the next to the last page and the recto of the last page. The covers for this edition, which were paper over boards, varied greatly, though all I saw used decorative papers printed in bright patterns with a white label printed in black and an ornamental border at the top and bottom. Size: 7-1/4 x 5-1/4. Printed and published by Leonard and Virginia Woolf at the Hogarth Press, Hogarth House, Richmond, 1922.

This is the usual sort of book produced by the Woolfs in the early stages of the Press's history except for the unusual variation in bindings of which there may be more than the four I have seen so far. The ink is fairly black, the spacing good, the margins generous. Virginia noted in her diary that no one bought *Daybreak* and copies were still available in 1939.[12]

Roger Fry's friend Robert C. Trevelyan was also a frequent guest at the Woolfs'. They published his work continually through the history of the Press, adding seven titles by him to their list, although only one was handprinted. Trevelyan was a poet and a translator of Lucretius, educated at Trinity College and an Apostle. He was a particular friend of G.E. Moore, which would have endeared him to Leonard. He was a great talker and both Woolfs enjoyed his company. He was a rather absorbing person who once scorched the bottom of his trousers standing before a fire at the Woolfs' home in Richmond while reading his poems aloud.[13]

> *Poems and Fables.* By R.C. Trevelyan. 23 pages, uncut. This book is dedicated to Linda and Aubrey Waterfield. There is a table of contents. A large version of Bell's wolf's head appears at the end of the book as a colophon and "The Hogarth Press" does not appear on the title page or elsewhere in the book. The cover is multi-colored, marbled, paper-covered boards. The label is cream printed in black within a double frame (outer line thick, inner thin). Size: 8-3/4 x 5-1/2. Printed and published by Leonard and Virginia Woolf at 52 Tavistock Square, London W.C., 1925.

Virginia wrote to R.C. Trevelyan about this book in January 1925:

> We would like to print your poems, and think we ought to keep it a small book, which we could print ourselves . . . . As it is, of course we can't bind ourselves to have it done by any particular time. But this is only to say that we should like to do it, and details can wait. (Letter to R.C. Trevelyan, January 1925)

It is a good example of the books printed by the Woolfs from the middle years of the Press: good layout, fairly good black ink, no typographical difficulties to bother the typesetter.

The last book I will discuss in this chapter is a quiet, special book which was so private that John Lehmann did not list it in the *Complete Catalogue of the Hogarth Press*, published in 1939 after he took over the partnership from Virginia. He may not even have known it existed.

Cecil Nathan Sidney Woolf was the fourth of Leonard's brothers and, like him, educated at Trinity College. He was preparing for a career in law when the First World War broke out and by January 1915 was in the cavalry with his brother Philip. The incident which killed Cecil and left Philip badly hurt was called "characteristic of the 1914 War" by Leonard when he retold the story in *Beginning Again.*[14] Cecil was not a great poet, but as for so many others from his generation of educated men, his youthful poems were the only fruit of his short life, and like many other families with similar losses in the war, the Woolfs published Cecil's poems as a private tribute to his memory.

Poems. By C.N. Sidney Woolf, late 20th Hussars (Spec. Res.). Fellow of Trinity College, Cambridge. Unpaginated and uncut. The foreword and dedication are by P.S.W. [Philip Sidney Woolf]. The cover is a soft white paper wrapper with yapped edges, printed in black. Size: 5-3/8 x 4-1/4. Hogarth Press, Richmond.

This little book of nineteen pages was the second book printed by the Woolfs. It is a fragile volume of utter simplicity. Though obvious care was taken in printing it, the paper is too soft for clean printing. The cover overlaps the body with yapp edges giving an even more delicate appearance to this book.

"I can't think what happened to our telephone—it was working alright this end. However, I could hardly have come, we've been working on a book of Cecil Woolf's poems and only just got them done" (Letter to Vanessa Bell, 19 March 1918). The Woolfs were so intent upon printing this book that they interrupted the printing of *Prelude*, eventually published in May 1918, to print and distribute it privately.

4

Books by Acquaintances

This chapter shows how broad was the circle with which the Woolfs had contacts and from which they received material to print. Though here, as in the next chapter, "Books by Worthy Unknowns," it is probable that much of the communication took place over the telephone, making the exact connection between the Woolfs and an author difficult to define, in general, it can be assumed that the more personal the author's association was with the Woolfs, the more likely it is that important conversations would have been mentioned by Virginia in her letters or her diary.

There are many ways in which the Woolfs might have met or at least learned of Theodora Bosanquet, though the exact circumstances are not known. She was educated at University College, University of London. Early in her career, she acted as secretary to Henry James, from 1907 until his death in 1916. Both Leonard and Virginia were greatly impressed by James. He was a close friend of Leslie Stephen and after the latter's death, James' friendship with Virginia continued. She makes a number of references to him in her writings. Leonard writes at length on James and his influence on the young Cambridge men of 1900 in his book *Growing*, which covers that period. After James' death, Bosanquet served in the War Trade Intelligence Department and then as assistant to the secretary of the Ministry of Food. In 1920, she became the executive secretary of the International Federation of University Women, at a time when higher education for women was still uncommon. It is possible that John Maynard Keynes knew Bosanquet since both were in government at the same time, and he could have introduced her to his friends the Woolfs. Virginia's interest in education was also of long standing, starting when she watched her brothers go off to university and including her own teaching at Morley College and the writing of *A Room of One's Own*, a book Bosanquet admired.[1] Any of these common interests would have made the Woolfs aware of Theodora Bosanquet and interested in her.

When she is first mentioned in a letter from Virginia to the artist Gerald Brenan, Virginia mistakenly calls her an American, "astute and bold."[2] This description must have been apt; we know, for instance, from Leon Edel that Bosanquet was determined to work for James, whom she did not know, and when she learned that he needed a typist, she "promptly set herself to learn typing."[3] The impression given in the Brenan letter is that Bosanquet sent her material unsolicited to the Woolfs, which was usually the case for the commercial side of the Press after it had been established a few years.

In February of 1924, Virginia wrote directly to Bosanquet about an article of 10,000 words on James for which the Press would pay her twenty-five percent of the profits: "I think it should make a most interesting little book."[4] This is a business letter and attests to the fact that the Woolfs wanted the article for their first series of Hogarth Essays, which was made up of four titles all published in 1924. Of these, Bosanquet's *Henry James at Work* was the only title handprinted.

> *Henry James at Work*. By Theodora Bosanquet. 33 pages, cut. Hogarth Essays, first series, no. 3. The cover is a cream paper wrapper printed in green with a series title and pamphlet title and the authors printed above an illustration of a person reading a large book (the cover varies in the other titles in this series); it is initialed by Vanessa Bell, with the publisher's statement below. Size: 8-3/8 x 5-1/2. Printed and published by Leonard and Virginia Woolf at the Hogarth Press, 52 Tavistock Square, London, 1924.

It is not known why the Woolfs handprinted this pamphlet, but since they printed only one other book that year, perhaps they just wanted to keep a finger in their hobby. The format is the right size for their hand press but the type is too crowded, the inking so badly done that the blank places render the text nearly indecipherable. The copious footnotes are in italics, also crowded, and almost impossible to read. The worst fault, however, is the poorly aligned type, which bleeds into the verso page and shadows the type there. Bosanquet, with her meticulous secretarial skills, must have been quite chagrined at the form her essay took in the hands of the Woolfs.

According to Leonard, all the pamphlets in the series had their merits, and he goes into his views on the subject thoroughly in *Downhill All the Way*. The subject of Bosanquet's pamphlet would certainly have had great appeal and, in fact, it is listed in the 1939 catalogue as a second edition.

Nancy Cunard was a British poet, writer and printer. In Edwardian England, she was part of an exuberant trio with Lady Diana Manners, later Lady Duff Cooper, and Iris Tree, a friend of Dora Carrington's at the Slade School and daughter of Beerbolm Tree. Together they dashed through the gay life of London and Paris. Like her mother, an American who changed her name from Maud to Emerald and led a mad section of London society in the early 1900s, Cunard was always an exception to the rule. Her friends were legion. She was painted by Kokoschka and Wyndham Lewis, photographed by Cecil Beaton and Man Ray, sculpted by Brancusi, and authors Aldous Huxley and Michael Arlen created characters based on her personality. In the thirties, Cunard honored black culture with one of the first anthologies of miscellany from its art and literature by publishing *Negro*. She went to Spain to report on the Spanish Civil War for the *Manchester Guardian*. Cunard's poetry was first published in Edith Sitwell's *Wheels, An Anthology of Verse*, which took its title from one of Cunard's poems. Other works by Cunard include *GM, Memories of George Moore* (who might have been her father) and *These Were the Hours*, a history of her private press.

Needless to say, with this activity the Woolfs and Nancy Cunard would have been bound to cross paths sooner or later, even if they had not known her from childhood. Leonard does not mention her in his memoirs, but in a marvelous tribute published in *Nancy Cunard, Brave Poet, Indomitable Rebel 1895-1965* he offers the following reflection, which also sums up the views of the fifty people included with him:

> She seemed to drift in and out, in and out of one's room and one's life; but she was always the same Nancy, unlike anyone else in the world. When she was young, she was enchanting and though she lost, like all living things from daffodils to puppies to les jeunes filles en fleur, the ravishing freshness of youth, she never lost that strange quality of enchantment. I had from the moment I saw her a great affection for her and she had, I think, an affection for me.[5]

Parallax. By Nancy Cunard. 24 pages, uncut. There is a note by the author thanking the artist, Eugene McCrown, for his drawings in the dedication space. The cover is off-white paper-covered boards printed in black with one drawing on the front, incorporating the title and author into the design, and a second on the back. Size: 9 x 5-5/8. Printed and published by Leonard and Virginia Woolf at the Hogarth Press, 52 Tavistock Square, London, 1925.

This is a finely printed booklet, simple in design, with one of the few poems published by the Woolfs in a modern style with varying lines and typefaces used for emphasis. Hope Mirrlees' *Paris*, which is discussed later in this chapter, is another example. *Parallax* also uses the larger format of the two sizes generally found among the handprinted books. The margins are generous and the type is fairly black. The binding is neat, though a little too tight. Of the several copies I saw, one was partly opened and others were quite worn on the top edge and along the spine. The artist, Eugene McCrown, was a friend of Cunard's, and little or nothing is written about him in the usual art references. He was a Canadian, active in the early 1920s.

There is no telling how the Woolfs came to Robert Graves' attention or he to theirs, but the paths around Garsington's decorative pool are strewn with conversations mentioning both parties. The Woolfs were interested in Graves and his work before they ever met him. He went right into the war from school and emerged an officer, though he suffered severe wounds which may have left him mentally unstable. When Graves entered Oxford in 1919, as an older student, he was married to feminist Nancy Nicholson and already established as a noted poet with three publications behind him. He belongs to that small band of war poets epitomized by Edmund Blunden who survived and lived afterwards with varying degrees of success in the shadow of that experience. Others such as Siegfried Sassoon, Frank Prewitt and Herbert Read (the latter two printed by the Woolfs) are part of Graves' story because diaries and memoirs from the period show that all these poets knew one another either from the trenches or through publications or perhaps from weekend gatherings at Garsington.

Graves has remained a controversial figure since he began appearing in print. His personal life was bizarre and his relationship with Laura Riding, also printed by the Woolfs, forms only one extraordinary episode. With Riding, Graves wrote *A Survey of Modernist Poetry* in 1927 and founded the Seizin Press which they moved to Majorca in 1929, where they continued their unconventional creative partnership for the next decade.

Virginia records that she first met Graves in April of 1925 when she found him "goggling at the door" and mistook him for "some *Nation* genius."[6] By this time he may have been, since he was definitely reviewing for Leonard by 1926 when Leonard had to talk the poet Roy Campbell out of fighting Graves over a review. The Woolfs had already published two of his books before Virginia met him, one of which was his poem *The Feather Bed*, which he asked them to print.[7] Eventually, the Press published six works of poetry and criticism by Graves.

The Feather Bed. By Robert Graves with a cover designed by William Nicholson. 28 pages, uncut. The text includes an "Introductory letter to John Ransome [sic] the American Poet" by Graves. Edition notes have been tipped in facing the title page. The cover, as noted on the title page, is a design by William Nicholson, unsigned, on the front and back, of black plumes on a pink paper-covered board, surrounding an open field of black where the title and author are printed in white; there is a black spine. The body is printed on a distinctly textured, laid paper. Size: 9-7/8 x 6-7/8. Printed and published by Leonard & Virginia Woolf at the Hogarth Press, Hogarth House, Richmond, 1923.

The style of *The Feather Bed* is similar to other early books, such as

Forster's *Pharos and Pharillon*, also of 1923, where in parts of the book the specific desires of the author become muddled because of the Woolfs' unsure printing skills and stylistic tastes. Here, half-titles in italic introduce not only the poem but also the introduction to John Crowe Ransom, whose name neither party seems to have realized was incorrectly spelled. The uneven printing is made worse by the heavily textured laid paper. There are no endpapers and in some copies I reviewed, the glue used to fix the body to the boards had slopped over the last page of the text, causing it to adhere to the back board. It would not be surprising if the reader became frustrated with this jumble and gave up his or her attempt to read Graves' poem, described by Virginia as "in the style of Browning."[8] In fact, several copies I saw were unopened or only partly opened.

Graves must have learned about Ransom at Oxford, where the latter had been a Rhodes scholar from 1910 to 1913. At Oxford Graves also met T.E. Lawrence, who interested him in private presses and introduced him to Ezra Pound, who certainly knew Ransom's poems, and whose acquaintance led Graves into the London literary world. The illustrator for *The Feather Bed*, William Nicholson, was Graves' father-in-law and a contemporary of Roger Fry. He attended the Académie Julian in Paris and began his career as a poster designer and book illustrator; his woodcuts won a gold medal at the 1900 Paris Exposition Universelle. All the Nicholson family were quite talented and independent people. William's son, Ben, was an innovative painter of abstract landscapes and made notable contributions to British art during the first half of this century. William Nicholson also designed the cover for Robert Graves' *Mock Beggar Hall*, published by the Press in 1924. Since Nicholson was a founding member of the National Portrait Society in London, it would be interesting to know if he also did the small likeness of Voltaire used as a frontispiece for Riding's *Voltaire*, printed by the Woolfs in 1927.

It is fairly well established that Lytton Strachey introduced Katherine Mansfield to Virginia in November of 1916 after he had met her at Garsington. When he first mentions a meeting, Virginia says she knows of Mansfield but had not met her nor read her work.[9] The meeting of these two writers and its implications for modern British literature have been extensively explored and the evidence gone over thoroughly in the course of subtle arguments concerning their mutual creative influence. The relationship between the two, taken at any level, is a study in the complexities of the literary and social currents of London during the years of the First World War. The publication of *Prelude* was something both wanted very much and its history is almost as well documented by the Woolfs in their writings as is that of *Two Stories*. Since Mansfield had had only one other book published, and that in 1911, she was naturally anxious to get this work into print and she too details the history of its publication in her writings. By a strange coincidence, *Prelude* is a memorial statement to her brother, Leslie Heron Beauchamp, who died in the war along with Cecil Woolf, whose memorial volume of poems interrupted its printing at the Press. The work is dedicated to Beauchamp and John Middleton Murry, with whom Mansfield was living at this time. Beauchamp's death turned Mansfield's thoughts back to her homeland of New Zealand and *Prelude* is one of several stories she set there.

> *Prelude.* By Katherine Mansfield. 68 pages, uncut. It is dedicated to "LHB and JMM." The cover has a stiff dark blue wrapper with yapp edges which has been sewn, glued and stapled. It is printed in black with title and author; a few copies were printed with a woodcut on the front and one on the back by J.D. Fergusson, unsigned and unacknowledged. Size: 8-1/2 x 6. Hogarth Press, Richmond.

The printing of this story forced the Woolfs into a new league of printers which they were ill prepared to enter. They would either have to borrow a larger press or spend the rest of their lives printing two pages at a time on their small hand press. They immediately got help with the typesetting but found just as quickly, when Alix Sargent-Florence Strachey quit, that it was not everyone's idea of a pleasant afternoon. The Woolfs themselves had not quite gotten the hang of it, having printed only one short booklet, a bit of letterhead and some advertisements when they started on *Prelude*. It may be true, as the story is told by their first employee, that they thought type was set with forceps, not fingers.[10] It is clear from their early corrections that it took the Woolfs a while to realize that the forceps were for picking out wrong type and making corrections in the line without tearing up the whole frame.

These problems were soon overcome, but the mystery remains as to why the Woolfs rejected J.D. Fergusson's illustrations for the cover after printing a handful of them. Born in Scotland, Fergusson gave up medicine for painting under the influence of Arthur Melville of the Glasgow School. Fergusson visited Paris around 1896 and again in 1898; he settled there in 1907 and taught at the Atelier de la Palette, where he would have met Grant and the Bells among other English art enthusiasts, and John Middleton Murry, who was also living in Paris. Fergusson became art editor of *Rhythm*, founded by Murry and Mansfield in 1911. For some reason, Virginia took a dislike to the designs for *Prelude*, which show a cheerful woman framed with flowers and broad leaves on the front and the same woman on the back, with wilted flowers. Fergusson is a minor but not unknown artist and he was certainly well known among Vanessa's crowd and well respected by his colleagues. In 1918 he was living on the same street as Mansfield, when she asked him to do the designs.

Other technical problems in *Prelude* are common in the early books. The paper cover is designed to overlap the body and in time this edge folds and the heavy paper, poor quality to begin with, deteriorates, and the covers break away, the spine weakens and it all crumbles. At this stage in their binding experience, the Woolfs were using all their know-how simply to hold the books together and they ended up with tight backs which destroyed the books when they were opened and read. The dark blue cover, printed in black, is unreadable. Considering the conditions under which Leonard printed this book—carrying chases to McDermott's shop after Virginia had set them in the dining room—it is amazing that the book can be read at all. Virginia's diary says:

> I can't fill up the lost days though it is safe to attribute them to printing. The title page was finally done on Sunday. Now I'm in the fury of folding & stapling, so as to have all ready for gluing & sending out tomorrow & Thursday. By rights these processes should be dull; but its always possible to devise some little skill or economy & the pleasure of profitting by them keeps one content. (*Diary*, 9 July 1918)

Leonard's says: "When I look at my copy of *Prelude* today, I am astonished at our courage and energy in attempting it and producing it only a year after we had started to teach ourselves to print."[11] It was an ambitious second attempt by a couple of amateur printers but the results are noble.

Mention must be made at this point of Middleton Murry's connection with the Press and the book it published for him, his poem *The Critic in Judgement*, which came out in 1919. Woolmer describes it in his *Checklist* of the Hogarth Press as printed by McDermott at the Prompt Press, but in Appendix II he lists it as handprinted by the Woolfs.[12] Leonard comments on Murry's book in a footnote to a discussion of when the Press began its commercial publishing: "In 1919 we had had Middleton Murry's *Critic in Judgement* printed for us by a small printer, my friend McDermott, but he and I really printed it together, and we printed only 200 copies. Virginia and I bound it."[13]

As usual, Leonard leaves a great deal unsaid, even when he bothers to footnote a point. The Woolfs detested Murry for his manners and because they thought his influence on Mansfield was detrimental to her creative genius. Leonard probably used this opportunity to practice his technique in using the bigger press at McDermott's. Since the Woolfs do not claim to have printed this book on the title page, it is not being considered in detail in this study.

The Woolfs probably met Hope Mirrlees before Virginia started to keep a diary in 1915. Virginia's letters mention Mirrlees' companion Jane Harrison, a noted classical scholar, as far back as 1904 when she encountered her at Cambridge. Virginia herself had made a study of the classics, both literature and language, and knew Harrison's work in the field. Mirrlees' friendship with

Virginia's sister-in-law, Karen Costelloe Stephen, and through her the friendship with the Woolfs, illustrate again the web of overlapping acquaintances which surrounds every new individual in this study. The Woolfs were certainly well enough disposed toward Mirrlees to entertain her and her mother in Richmond. Mirrlees found the Press:

> delightfully intimate & amateurish. When I was staying with them [the Woolfs] on one occasion . . . I asked if I might see the Hogarth Press, expecting to be taken to a room full of mysterious machinery. We were in the dining-room when I asked & they pointed to something behind my chair about the size of a radio, and informed me that that was the Hogarth Press.[14]

When the Woolfs asked Mirrlees "to write us a story," she sent them her poem *Paris*, composed while she was in Paris with Harrison in 1919.[15]

> *Paris*, a poem. By Hope Mirrlees. 23 pages, cut. This work is dedicated "A/Notre Dame de Paris/en Reconnaissance/ des Graces Accordees," printed on the verso of the title page in caps and framed with a heavy box which has been pressed, and the ink has bled through onto the title page, marring the surface and confusing its composition. The text, corrected in black ink by Virginia, is a great mixture of typefaces, language, non-language single letters, lines in upper or all lower case, erratic spacing, etc. Page 18 has two lines of music; page 22 (which is unnumbered) has the Big Dipper outlined in asterisks at the bottom of the page. It is followed by an address and date in colophon form which seems to refer to the author's residence in Paris and is probably the ending of the poem. The date is printed as "1916" but has been corrected by hand to "1919." The cover is a paper wrapper, printed with a gold, blue and red diamond design, glued around the signatures, which are sewn; there are no endpapers. The paper used for the body is poor quality, too soft to print clearly. The label is white, printed in red. Size: 6 x 4-1/2. Printed by Leonard & Virginia Woolf at the Hogarth Press, Paradise Road, 1919.

This book is the first example of the early Press books in which the text almost cries out "you asked for it" to the would-be printers. Surely only a true friend would bother to print the hodge-podge of constructions and symbols which make up *Paris* and which may or may not have made sense to the printers even after it came out right-side up and turned around on the page after being set. *Paris* is the worst example, but the poems *The Waste Land* and *Parallax* and Forster's book *Pharos and Pharillon* with its mixture of prose, dialogue, poetry and footnotes provide other kinds of typographical horrors for the typesetter and layout designer. The time and effort involved make these productions very expensive and most commercial publishers would not be able to take the chance on getting their investment back by mistaking public taste, particularly with unknown authors.

The Woolfs published despite this consideration in a deliberate attempt to give such forms of expression and unknown talent a chance. They were dedicated enough to their concept and to their authors to take on the rigors of printing these complicated literary compositions. Faced with the proof of their effort, one is again impressed by their determination and driving need for this strenuous activity in their otherwise rather cerebral existence.

Of Mirrlees, Virginia writes:

> she knows Greek and Russian better than I do French, is Jane Harrison's favourite pupil, and has written a very obscure, indecent and brilliant poem which we are going to print. (Letter to Margaret Llewelyn Davies, 17 August 1919)

While printing the poem, she writes in her diary for 24 April 1920 that she is "half blind with writing notices & corrections in 160 copies of Paris a poem by Hope Mirrlees." The date of this entry and others show that *Paris* was actually published in May of 1920, indicating once again the Woolfs' disregard for bibliographically correct details such as a true publication date. Since Virginia was thinking of publication when she wrote her letter in August of 1919, it is possible that the poem was printed in 1919 but not actually published until the following year.

In general, *Paris* conforms to the early results of the inexperienced printers and shows the characteristics common to the early books: it is roughly printed, with some technically inappropriate choices in layout, but is overall a charming and delightfully conceived publication, irritating in its execution.

Though Virginia does not mention Edwin Muir in her personal writings, Leonard remembers him fondly:

> He was so sensitive, intelligent and honest minded that, as a serious critic he always had something of his own worth saying even about masterpieces buried long ago under mountains and monuments of criticism. But even in the ephemeral and debased form of criticism, reviewing, he was remarkable. For a long time he used to review novels for me in the *Nation*, a mechanized, mind-destroying occupation for most people. For him, it never became mechanical and his mind's eye was as clear and lively after a year of it as when he began.[16]

Muir was known for most of his life as a critic and it was not until his collected works were published in 1952 that wider recognition was gained for his poetry. The Hogarth Press gave generous support to Muir, publishing most of his significant works, including his *First Poems* in 1925 and his only novel, *The Marionette*, as well as three books of criticism. One of his most significant collections, *Chorus of the Newly Dead*, was handprinted by the Woolfs in 1926.

Chorus of the Newly Dead. By Edwin Muir. 16 pages, uncut. Incorporates the small wolf's head on the title page as a printer's device and is dedicated to John Holms. The cover, which is both glued and sewn, is a marbled paper wrapper in black, orange, red and pink. The label is yellow printed in black within a double frame (outer line thick, inner thin). There are no endpapers. Size: 8-3/8 x 5-3/8. Printed & published by Leonard & Virginia Woolf at the Hogarth Press, London, 1926.

This book is much like the other books from the middle period of the Woolfs' printing history. It is distinguished by the marbled paper, the wolf's head by Bell and the larger, open-faced type. The publication statement includes both upper and lower case and the ampersand used freely, which here means everywhere possible. The middle publications all show this control over text and layout, with the neatness of binding and title page expected in a handcrafted book. The printing continues too gray for most tastes. In general, these books lack the added extras of some of the more demanding books produced in the earlier days with their half-titles, headings, various type forms and several languages, which the Woolfs came to handle well.

Leonard does not mention Herbert Read in his autobiographies but the two men had politics and an interest in art in common. Read's major contribution to British aesthetics was as a spokesman for the arts but he was also a poet and wrote and published continually, starting just after the First World War. His third book, *Mutations of the Phoenix*, was printed by the Woolfs in 1923. They also published *In Retreat*, which is a discussion of trench warfare, and *Phases of English Poetry*, which is still in print.

Mutations of the Phoenix. By Herbert Read. 51 pages, cut. A heavy laid paper with a pronounced watermark is used throughout the book, both for text and endpapers. Advertisements are printed on the last three pages with the last poem printed on the recto of the first advertisement page. The cover is red marbled paper-covered boards with a cloth spine and either red, maroon or blue. The narrow label on the spine is white with black printing, rules at the top and bottom with a decorative type separating the title from the author. Size: 9-7/8 x 7-3/8. Printed and published by Leonard & Virginia Woolf at the Hogarth Press, Hogarth House, Richmond, 1923.

This book is from the early period and all the elements are well handled including several languages. The rough textured paper made printing difficult and the inking is too pale and uneven.

It is now our plan (a day old) to walk from 2 to 3; print from 3 to 5; delay our tea; and so make headway. In fact, I set up a little of Read. (*Diary,* 10 February 1923)

Though *Mutations* still has the amateurish look of the early publications showing an inexperience in choosing materials for instance, it also reflects the Woolfs' interest in design with the decorative label.

Laura Riding Jackson is an American writer, poet, novelist and literary critic. When she moved to Europe in 1926 she left a husband named Gottschalk and almost immediately moved into Robert Graves' household. She returned to the United States in 1939 and married Jackson. Riding's biography seems to have been rewritten each time she entered a new relationship, so the Woolfs should be excused for confusing her names several times. Riding began publishing her poems in magazines in 1923 and was an early associate of John Crowe Ransom and the poets who sponsored the *Fugitive* magazine and developed the agrarian poem. The Hogarth Press published two long poems by Riding: *The Chaplet* in 1926 and in 1927 *Voltaire, A Biographical Fantasy*, which is still in print.

> *Voltaire, A Biographical Fantasy*. By Laura Riding Gottschalk. (The "Gottschalk" is overprinted on the title page with double bars of 6-point rules.) 30 pages, cut. There is a frontispiece unsigned (probably by William Nicholson), a small portrait of Voltaire. The work is dedicated to "L.G." (probably Riding's husband). The foreword, dated 1921, ends with a quote from Voltaire. The cover is a heavy black paper wrapper, glued over the sewn signatures, without endpapers. The label is cream printed in black with the title and "Laura Riding" in a double frame (outer line thick, inner thin). Size: 8-1/8 x 5-3/8. Printed & published by L. and V. Woolf at the Hogarth Press, 52 Tavistock Square, 1927.

The most startling aspect of this production is the willingness of the Woolfs to publish the title page with a double rule across Riding's married name. Instead of resetting the page, which would not have been a major task, the Woolfs for some inexplicable reason were satisfied with this response to some whim of Riding's, attempting to disassociate herself from her husband. However, since she did not bother to change the dedication, there is an air of haste about the proceedings which indicates that the printing schedule may have been too advanced to alter very much but the most obvious indication of her marriage. The alteration is shattering for the reader, who immediately confronts this violation against the whole tone of the book in the amused glance of Voltaire from the frontispiece. The poem is such a light-hearted, mock-serious discourse with even more mocking footnotes that the violation becomes very provoking. The depth of the Woolfs' aesthetic callousness is astonishing. In all other respects, the book is a fine example of a simply designed book enlivened by the artistic detail of an illustration or a single printer's embellishment. *Voltaire* has a complex text which the Woolfs handled quite well.

The title page does have its amusing side when Laura Riding's attitude toward her name is borne in mind. Within days of her arrival in London, Graves had brought her to Tavistock Square. Virginia writes that she entertained Graves and "Nancy Gottshalk," misspelling her name and confusing it with that of Graves' wife Nancy Nicholson.[17] When she comes to mention printing *Voltaire* in her diary, Virginia manages to confuse both names in the same passage:

> But I would like to learn to write a steady plain narrative style. Then perhaps I could catch up with the last few weeks; describe . . . how I stood in the basement printing Gottshalk with a great sense of shade & shelter. I like the obscure anonymity of the Press better a good deal than I like *Voltaire* by Riding. (*Diary,* 6 June 1927)

From Virginia's point of view neither the author nor the manuscript were terribly significant. What she enjoyed most was the satisfaction which came from the process of printing and making books.

In all fairness to the Woolfs, it should be mentioned that when they published Riding's first book, *The Chaplet,* the year before *Voltaire,* the author's name was "Laura Riding Gottschalk" and it was probably like that on the 1926 manuscript too. Riding simply changed her mind at the last minute.

In the mid-1930s, Dorothy Wellesley was "discovered" by W.B. Yeats and one of the consequences of their friendship, aside from publication of their correspondence, was the inclusion by Yeats of Wellesley and, probably through her, Sackville-West, in his anthology *The Oxford Book of Modern Verse* published in 1936. As a matter of fact, he gives more space to Wellesley than to himself or T.S. Eliot, which may surprise some people less familiar with Yeats' critical eye.

Wellesley, Duchess of Wellington, was a poet, editor and patron of British literature and art. She was born into the privileged class, as were Nancy Cunard and Vita Sackville-West. Wellesley is known mainly for her support of poets and artists in England between the wars and for her biographies of English Romantic poets, some of which are still in print. Bell and Grant decorated her homes and found other patrons through her introductions.

Virginia met Wellesley in 1922 while visiting Sackville-West, who was a close friend and to whom she dedicated her long poem *The Land.* The diaries and letters from that time show the development of the Woolfs' friendship with Wellesley, which never, however, became close. Though Leonard needed and appreciated her sponsorship of the Hogarth Living Poets through two series, he did not like the aristocratic Wellesley and she is not mentioned in his memoirs. The Press did publish one anthology and three books of her poetry; one they hand set.

Jupiter and the Nun. By Dorothy Wellesley. Unpaginated and uncut. Dedicated to "my daughter on her birthday, Dec. 26, 1931." The cover is marbled paper-covered boards in shades of blue printed in dark blue. The book is one four-page signature sewn but not glued. The endpapers are made of the same marbled paper as the cover. It is published as a signed, limited edition. Size: 8-3/4 x 6-3/4. Printed & published by Leonard & Virginia Woolf at the Hogarth Press, London, 1932.

This is the last of the thirty-four handprinted books by the Woolfs and is nearly as far in concept and execution as one can imagine from *Two Stories.* It is beautifully designed and printed; the materials are all fine quality. The sentiment, expressed in the dedication, is in keeping with the purpose of a traditional private press book: a gift, a special expression of gratitude or a token of one's affection. The content is merely a part of the design, conveniently short to form an especially delicate and exquisite booklet, as opposed to the first book from the Press, which was rough-hewn from type and paper to give form and being to the individual stories created by the Woolfs.

By the time *Jupiter and the Nun* was printed, the Woolfs were finding the Press a constant source of irritation. After many years of fighting its demands, they completely gave up the printing in 1932. The Woolfs had been reducing their printing load for several years by printing fewer books and letting the apprentice printers in the shop do more of the work. From 1927, with Riding's *Voltaire*, they published only one handprinted book annually, except in 1931 when they printed the three pages of *Sissinghurst* and Rylands' twenty-four page *Poems.* After publishing the unknown Stanley Snaith's *A Flying Scroll* in 1928, the Woolfs published only close friends and associates and Virginia's book, *On Being Ill*, in 1930, eleven years after *Kew Gardens.*

5

Books by Worthy Unknowns

I have called the authors in this chapter "worthy unknowns" because their exact relationship with the Woolfs cannot be established from the Woolfs' testimony. Nothing that would be enlightening about them is mentioned by either Leonard or Virginia, if they are mentioned at all in the autobiographies, or the diaries or letters. With few exceptions, these people have also remained outside the scope of anthologies, dictionaries and literary histories of twentieth-century British literature, and very little is known about any of them, except John Crowe Ransom, beyond the barest facts. What is certain is that, at one point, the Woolfs were sufficiently interested in them to put energy into producing their poems by hand and publishing them with the almost sure knowledge that the books were not going to pay for themselves but could only be carried through the success of the commercial side of the Hogarth Press.

Ena Limebeer is an enigma in that she is totally unknown and, it seems, unknowable. No biographical details have been discovered about her; not even her dates are given with the listing of her works in the catalogues for the British Museum and the Library of Congress. More intriguing still is that Leonard, who mentions very few of these authors at all, mentions Limebeer twice, though he does not bother to index her name.[1] Both times he mentions her poems in connection with the Press in an off-hand manner that suggests she should be familiar to his reading audience. No one, however, in the major research libraries in this country with extensive collections of British literature and a specific interest in the Hogarth Press knows who she was, though they all have at least one copy of *To a Proud Phantom*. She published poems in the *New Age*, which also published Katherine Mansfield's work, the *New Leader*, the *Nation*, where Leonard was literary editor during this period, the *New Statesman*, where an old Cambridge friend of Leonard's, Desmond McCarthy, was literary editor at this time, and in the *Saturday Westminster Gazette*. These publications are recognized as having granted permission for the Press to reprint Limebeer's poems in *To a Proud Phantom*. Limebeer also wrote *Market Town* (London, Jonathan Cape, 1931) and *The Dove and the Roe Buck* (London, J.M. Dent, 1932; New York, Dutton, 1933).

A fair guess is that Limebeer was a part of the newly educated class of women either from Cambridge, as was Virginia's sister-in-law Karen Stephen and her cousin Fredegond Shove, or from Oxford, as was Dorothy Sayers, or from the University of London, where Theodora Bosanquet received her degree. Periodicals made space for these women writers. Basil Blackwell, among other booksellers, published as well as sold books and one of his literary efforts was the series "Young Poets Unknown to Fame," which for a time was edited by Sayers and where, it may be recalled, Shove's first book of poetry was published. Sayers was also connected by friendship to an editor of *Time and Tide*, which leads one back to the Hogarth Press through Theodora Bosanquet, who was also associated with that publication from its inception.

The literary world of London at that time, as now, had many levels and a variety of information channels, and for this select group of women, from whom of course Virginia was excluded by age and lack of a formal education, it must have had its own kind of "referral system" and rumor mills. Limebeer may have been a teacher who also wrote, or a literary professional like Sayers, or like Shove, the wife of an intellectual who also wrote. There is one bit of tantalizing information which supports this general supposition but leads nowhere. While searching for Ena I discovered another Limebeer who is also a woman and seems to have been associated with Oxford. Dora E. Limebeer wrote at least one book which was published by Oxford University Press, *The Greeks and Romans*, a second edition of which was published in 1949. Unfortunately, the "E" stands for Emily, and unless "Ena" is a nickname or a pseudonym, she is not Leonard's Limebeer. Virginia does not mention her at all.

> *To a Proud Phantom.* By Ena Limebeer. 32 pages, uncut. Dedicated "to my father" and with a statement of reproduction rights. The cover is marbled paper-covered boards in pink, orange and blue with a white label printed in black. Size: 7-5/8 x 5-1/8. Printed and published by Leonard and Virginia Woolf at the Hogarth Press, Richmond, 1923.

This is a small, well-printed book of collected poems. It offered no text problems for the Woolfs and they executed the work with fair ability, which is not surprising since by the time they came to print this title, they had already printed more than a dozen others. Since *To a Proud Phantom* is so widely represented in collections of Hogarth Press publications in the United States, it must have had little commercial value, and been easily available to collectors; indeed it was still in print in 1939. Several copies I saw were only partly opened, always an indication that though bought, the book was not read.

Ruth Manning-Sanders is a poet, novelist and children's writer. She spent her childhood in Cheshire and the Scottish highlands and was educated at Manchester University, where she met her husband, author George Manning-Sanders. The couple appears to have escaped the obligations of the First World War by wandering around Britain in a horse-drawn caravan. Sometime during this period, Ruth worked for a few years with a circus, an experience she drew on several times for her children's books and for a history of the English circus. She has written nearly fifty books of poetry, folklore, fiction and stories for children as well as book reviews for the *London Mercury*, *Time and Tide*, the *Nation* and the *Athenaeum*. The Hogarth Press published two books by Manning-Sanders and both were hand set by the Woolfs.

The Woolfs seem to have been introduced to Manning-Sanders by their friend Katherine Cox Arnold-Forster, who encouraged the poet to send her material to the Press.

> Did I ever tell you about Mrs. Manning-Sanders, your friend? She sent us a long poem, which seems to have a good deal of merit, and we are going to bring it out this spring. (Letter to Katherine Arnold-Forster, 2 December 1921)

From Manning-Sanders' recollections the Woolfs emerge as encouraging and friendly; she liked them,

> especially Virginia, who was lying on a sofa . . . and who struck me as most beautiful. They were both friendly and couldn't have been more kind but I didn't see much of them. I was young at the time and had a strong instinct against getting mixed up with the Bloomsbury set.[2]

It is pretty obvious from Manning-Sanders' vagabond life that her sort of adventure was different than that of most of Virginia's acquaintances. One can imagine Virginia in her most charming way drawing from Manning-Sanders descriptions of these adventures and savoring the vicarious experience of being in a caravan or with the circus. Unfortunately what survives of Virginia's impression of Manning-Sanders is one of her clever, cutting remarks mixed with a sincere compliment which nearly removes the sting from her barbed wit:

> We are—Mr. Partridge and Leonard are—busy printing a new long poem by a short fat poetess, who came to correct her proofs the other day and stayed for 2 hours and a half, like a baby sucking a coral, discussing her genius. But she was very nice, and very modest. (Letter to Lady Robert Cecil, 6 February 1922)

Karn is another straightforward piece of printing.

Karn. By Ruth Manning-Sanders. 45 pages, cut. There is a listing of previously published books and forthcoming ones, including *Karn* and *Daybreak* which had already been published, on the verso of the last blank page. The cover is gold paper-covered boards with a red label printed in black. Size: 8-1/2 x 5-1/2. Printed and published by Leonard and Virginia Woolf at the Hogarth Press, Hogarth House, Richmond, 1922.

Karn did not offer the Woolfs any particular problems. It is a little too gray and the paper is not very good, but it all fits together well.

> Mrs. Manning-Sanders forges ahead. She has reached the printing off stage which means that Ralph works in the basement, and leaves the machine dirty. (*Diary*, 4 February 1922)

The second book printed by the Woolfs for Manning-Sanders also offered them no difficulties.

Martha-Wish-You-Ill. By Ruth Manning-Sanders. 16 pages, uncut. The small Bell wolf's head is used as a printer's device on the title page. The cover is a marbled paper wrapper in several colors with a cream label printed in black within a double frame (outer line thick, inner thin). The signatures are sewn and glued. Size: 8-3/8 x 5-1/2. Printed & published by Leonard & Virginia Woolf at the Hogarth Press, London, 1926.

Martha-Wish-You-Ill falls into the middle period of the Woolfs' printing venture and is the sort of book they produced with competence and individuality. However, Virginia notes with some weariness in her diary for 1926 a refrain which was to grow more familiar over the next five years:

> The publishing season is about to begin. Nessa says Why don't you give it up? I say, because I enjoy it. Then I wonder, but do I? What about Rome & Sicily? And Manning-Sanders is not worth the grind. (*Diary*, 23 February 1926.)

Earlier she had written to Sackville-West:

> Devil that you are, to vanish to Persia and leave me here; dabbling in wet type, which makes my fingers frozen; and setting up the poems of Mrs. Manning-Sanders, which the more I set them the less I like. (Letter to V. Sackville-West, 17 February 1926)

No one seems to have liked or recalled the title of this book either. When it was listed in the out-of-print section of the 1939 catalogue of the Press's books, it was listed as *Martha-Wish-You-Well* and in the *English Catalogue of Books* it is listed as *Martin-Wish-You-Ill.*

Herbert Edward Palmer was a former teacher, a poet and reviewer, educated at Birmingham University and Bonn University. He taught for twenty years in England, Germany and France before giving up teaching in 1921 to devote his time to writing, fly fishing and long-distance hill walking. His works include several books of poetry, two of which were published by the Hogarth Press, *Songs of Salvation, Sin & Satire*, handprinted by the Woolfs, and a limited edition of *The Armed Muse Poems*. The Press also published *The Judgement of François Villon, A Pageant-Episode Play in Five Acts*. Only Palmer's collection of criticism, *Post-Victorian Poetry*, is still in print.

It is not clear just how the Woolfs made contact with Palmer or why the Press published three books for him. Probably they met him or his work through one of Sackville-West's various attempts to encourage poets between the wars or through Leonard's literary editorships.[3]

Songs of Salvation, Sin & Satire. By Herbert E. Palmer. 32 pages, uncut. The small wolf's head by Bell is used as a printer's device on the title page. It is dedicated to "the ghosts of John Masefield and Siegfried Sassoon." The cover is marbled paper-covered boards in reds and blues with a white label printed in black within a double frame (outer line thick, inner thin). Size: 8-1/2 x 5-1/2. Printed & published by Leonard and Virginia Woolf at the Hogarth Press, 52 Tavistock Square, London W.C. (n.d.).

The 1939 catalogue gives 1923 as the publication date of this book but in fact the preface and a letter from Virginia to Sackville-West place it in 1925:

> I am sure my printing Mr. Palmer's poems, as I did this Summer, gave him more intense pleasure than all the Common Readers and Mrs. Dalloways I shall ever write gave the rest of the world. (Letter to Sackville-West, 1 September 1925)

Perhaps Virginia was recalling the preface, in which Mr. Palmer took the opportunity to tell the reader where and how he could obtain Palmer's previously published books and how much each cost.

The book itself is a fine small book from the middle period containing rather ordinary poems and offering no particular technical problems for the Woolfs. Why they did not bother to put the publication date on the title page is anybody's guess; they exercised their usual free-wheeling sense of bibliographic informality by not bothering with a publication date and giving the title without an ampersand on the label and with one on the title page. They also seem to have enjoyed playing with upper and lower case type in both of the publication statements. The main question with this volume is how the Woolfs could bring themselves to print such drivel from such an unctuous and self-serving personality, conclusions which can be drawn from reading the book and which color one's response to Virginia's comment to Sackville-West. Can Palmer's relationship with Masefield and Sassoon have been close enough to allow him the breach of taste of his dedication? However, since both men were lively enough at the time to defend themselves if they had seen fit, our concern on this point is limited. But the question remains, why did the Woolfs bother with Palmer? What was Leonard's opinion? Was it merely a caprice on Virginia's part to please Sackville-West?

Frank Prewitt was born in Canada in 1893 and probably died there in 1962. When he is mentioned, which is infrequently, he is usually called "Toronto" and footnotes refer to him as a poet and farmer. His work has not been anthologized in books of Canadian poetry and he ceases to be mentioned sometime in the twenties in the recollections of his wartime friends, particularly Siegfried Sassoon and Ottoline Morrell. Unlike Sassoon, Read, Graves and others mentioned before in connection with the First World War, Prewitt does not seem to have made a successful re-entry into civilian life after returning from the front. He is mentioned as being at loose ends, without funds, and at one point unhappily married. He seems to have crossed and recrossed the Atlantic trying to find himself until he finally disappeared from literary circles. The British Museum lists three books by Prewitt: a novel, a collection of poems, and the book printed by the Woolfs which it lists as "*Poems* (Richmond, 1921)," indicating that it was published by the author himself.[4]

> *Poems.* By Frank Prewitt. Unpaginated, uncut. The cover is of a coated white paper wrapper printed in black. The title page repeats this exact layout without a publication statement; the verso of the title page has Printed and published for the author at the Hogarth Press. Richmond (n.d.)

It is a strange little book to have come from the Hogarth Press. It is personally printed by the Woolfs and in their style but it is not a personal book. Though it is listed in succeeding advertisements as a Hogarth Press publication, *Poems* is obviously a vanity book printed for the author and one wonders at whose expense. The self-effacing publication statement on the verso of the title page, and the very simple design and layout, one of the simplest by the Woolfs, along with Cecil Woolf's *Poems*—all these points add up to an odd book for the Woolfs. Prewitt's *Poems* is fairly well printed on laid paper, with only a few gray places, some bleeding and some unaligned passages, all common faults in the early books. The body of the book is sewn through the wrappers with the threads showing, as was the case with most of the earlier bindings, beginning with *Two Stories* and continuing until they began to use paper-covered boards. The only comment I found concerning this book was in a letter from Virginia to Lytton Strachey dated August 29, 1921: "The Literary Supt. by the way says that Prewitt is a poet; perhaps a great one." Be that as it may, the book was still available from the Press in 1939.

John Crowe Ransom was a noted American critic, editor and poet known for his association with the Southern Renaissance Movement. Ransom helped found the *Fugitive* which, as noted earlier, published work by Laura Riding. Published by the Hogarth Press, Ransom's *Grace after Meat* includes selections from *Poems about God* and *Chills and Fever*. Distinguished as John Crowe Ransom is, and as well known as he is to American readers of twentieth-century poetry, he is the only author of a handprinted book which neither Woolf mentions in writing. Why this is so may be explained by the fact that the Woolfs probably never met Ransom. He was, in all probability, brought to their attention by Robert Graves, who knew him or at least knew his work from Ransom's years at Oxford as a Rhodes scholar. Ransom's poetry would have been known to all the war poets who came down from the universities and went up the lines in 1914 and to others who were following the literary trends of the time. In any case, the Woolfs were ill-disposed toward Americans, particularly Virginia, who makes several nasty remarks about their general characteristics in her private writings. Whatever the reason, Ransom is not mentioned and thus there is no hint of what the Woolfs thought of him or his poetry beyond the bare fact that they bothered to set his poems and to spell his name correctly for *Grace after Meat*.

Grace After Meat. By John Crowe Ransom, with an introduction by Robert Graves. 57 pages, cut. The work is dedicated to Robert Graves. It has a table of contents. The cover is paper-covered boards in yellow with an overall design in white, green and red; the label is yellow printed in black within a single frame (thin lines). Size: 8-1/2 x 5-1/2. Printed & published by Leonard & Virginia Woolf at the Hogarth Press, 52 Tavistock Square, London W.C., 1924.

This book is a good example of the best of the early books, with its distinctive cover and shape. It has the technical problems found in other early works, though the text offered no challenges: inking uneven and too gray, poor paper for the body and for the cover, which has become brittle over the years. This book was still in print in 1939, which might say something for the rest of literary London's opinion of Ransom and American poets between the wars.

Stanley Snaith was a writer, librarian and mountain climber. His publications include several books of poetry, fiction and prose as well as many books on the history and excitement of mountain climbing. Snaith contributed scripts to the BBC, as did George Rylands and V. Sackville-West, and articles to such periodicals as the *Observer*, the *Listener* and the *London Mercury*. The Woolfs may have met Snaith through Rylands or Sackville-West but it is probably coincidental that Virginia's father was one of the most celebrated mountain climbers of the late nineteenth century. Whatever the Woolfs' connection with Snaith, they liked his work well enough to print two books for him: *April Morning* in 1926 and *A Flying Scroll* in 1928.

> *April Morning*. By Stanley Snaith. 24 pages, cut. The small Bell wolf's head is used as a printer's device for the title page. The acknowledgment for reprint rights states "from the Golden Hind" on the verso of the title page. The cover is a marbled paper wrapper in black with rust and brown. It is sewn and glued to the body without endpapers. The label is white printed in black within a double frame (outer line thick, inner thin). Size: 8-1/4 x 5-1/2. Printed & published by Leonard & Virginia Woolf at the Hogarth Press, London, 1926.

This is a neat publication from the middle period of the Press, pleasantly arranged and competently produced: the inking is good; the paper is good; the covers reflect the Woolfs' love of colorful wrappers, simply bound to the body.

> *A Flying Scroll*. By Stanley Snaith. 24 pages, cut. This work is dedicated to "my wife." There is a note which reads "Several poems which have appeared in the *Gramophone* and the *London Mercury* are reprinted in this book by courtesy of the respective editors." The cover is yellow paper-covered boards printed with an overall design of black dots over a background of white diamonds. The label is yellow printed in black within a double frame (outer line thick, inner line thin). Size: 7-1/2 x 5. Printed and published by Leonard and Virginia Woolf at the Hogarth Press, 52 Tavistock Square, London, W.C., 1928.

A Flying Scroll is very like other books from the middle period of the Woolfs' printing career, with slight variations.[5] There is no wolf's head on the title page; they have used no ampersands in the publication statement but the cover design has a flair characteristic of the best books from the Woolfs and it has the simplicity and competence of layout and execution which mark it as a fine private press book without the ostentatious display of craftsmanship which crept into *Sissinghurst* and *Jupiter and the Nun*.

6

The Woolfs and the Book Arts Tradition

When the Woolfs wandered up Farrington Street on a certain March afternoon in 1917, they were stopped by the windows of the Excelsior Printing Supply Company. Leonard recalls that moment:

> Nearly all the implements of printing are materially attractive and we stared through the window at them rather like two hungry children gazing at buns and cakes in a baker shop window. I do not know which of us first suggested that we should go inside and see whether we could buy a machine and type and teach ourselves.[1]

There are not many sensible reasons for buying a printing press and going into the publishing business. It is an expensive enterprise. The equipment is bulky and there is always the need for more of something—different typefaces, better papers and more room. It is very time consuming and it is only the first step if the object is to sell what is printed. Most private presses are started either because someone loves to print or he needs to publish. The book arts tradition is made of individuals who love to print, those whose satisfaction is in producing a well-made book, usually beautifully designed and easily readable. Often these people publish classic literary works to honor the beauty of the text by surrounding it with a fitting, personalized statement of the printer's admiration for the author's work. Publishing houses, on the other hand, encourage and support an author's ideas, investing in his books because the publisher thinks the public will pay to get his thoughts. A standardized system of book components is used to express these ideas clearly. The publishers' goal is to reach a large number of readers, spread the thoughts or creative genius of their authors and make a profit, avoiding the costs of a specialized production and the intellectual and emotional distractions of beautifully produced books which are more comparable to a work of art than a vehicle for thought. In short, publishers produce books to be bought and presumably read while private presses produce books to be admired, bought, and read.

As Leonard says, printing by hand is an attractive operation. The equipment and apparatus needed for it function with an almost toy-like fascination. Separate pieces of type fit into a composing stick which holds a line of words. Used with care, forceps lift individual letters from a line to correct inverted letters or substitute others in misspelled words. Each line is transferred to a chase and aligned with others. After spaces have been filled with "furniture," everything is tightened up to form an even body of type which is of course unreadable. It is turned around and backward in the line so that when printed the line will read from left to right, right side up. There is also something childishly satisfying about the messy process of inking, rolling and printing the type. When the result from the pulled page reveals a neat, clean, sensible composition, it is not unusual to hear little shouts of joy from the printer. The pride of mastering even the simplest application of this craft can still be felt by children of all ages. Roderick Cave has commented in *The Private Press* that the Woolfs' "episode was typical of thousands of the same sort since the introduction of Cowper's parlour Press three-quarters of a century earlier; where it differed from these was in the growth of the hobby into a distinguished publishing house."[2]

This was not the only exception in the Woolfs' experience with printing. The most typical Hogarth Press books have a joy and an abandonment of convention about them which leads one to appreciate the spirit of their creation even though the item itself may repel either consciously or unconsciously by its sloppy craftsmanship. Colin Franklin describes the Hogarth Press in his history of British private presses as a "bold" exception, "never passionate for good printing." He goes on to say "That it turned out the most interesting poems and stories of the century and had cover sketches by Vanessa Bell still does not bring it in. It bore less relation to the revival of printing than the Omega Workshops to Morris and Co."[3]

William Morris founded his interior design studio and factory in 1861, long before he set up the Kelmscott Press in the 1890s. Roger Fry made the Omega Workshops a direct antithesis to Morris, yet both men attempted to create objects that were more meaningful than those produced by the impersonal methods of the Industrial Revolution. Its lifeless products, mass-produced and untouched by a humanizing spirit, were prevalent in the nineteenth century and included everything from household goods to books. Morris, appalled by the situation he found prevailing aesthetically and spiritually in the goods and men who made them, tried to infuse life and spirit into the object by heightening the craftsmanship of the worker and instilling in him a pride of accomplishment while enhancing the quality of his product through better design and materials. Fry's philosophy was somewhat different. He felt the need to create more meaningful items too but believed that objects would take on the joy of their creation, expressing the pleasure an artist feels when he has satisfactorily fulfilled a creative impulse through an object, be it a chair, a pot or a textile. Meaning for him came not through the perfecting of a technique but in the opportunity to create. It is within this aesthetic that the Woolfs' attitude toward their printing and its end result must be seen. Where their hand has definitely been, in the earlier books, it is very clear to see. The later books which look out of character reflect a different hand; they are more the sort of book George Rylands and John Lehmann talked of producing should they ever found a press:

> Dadie [Rylands] had worked with the Woolfs as manager for a short period some years before and had been rescued from that not altogether happy experience by winning his fellowship at King's. During that time, he had helped the Woolfs in the actual printing of some of their booklets of poetry, and had found such pleasure in it that he had conceived the idea of buying a small press of his own. . . . I, who had become deeply interested in William Morris and all his works while at Eton, also had a secret wish to do just the same.[4]

Yet the Woolfs, as Cave remarks, "tried to produce their books well, but they were not in the least interested in producing fine books as such; their concern was with the text above all."[5] Or, as the grand old man of printing, Douglas C. McMurtrie, has wryly commented, "the Woolfs continued to divert themselves from time to time with efforts at typographic self-expression."[6] The extraordinary aspect of the Woolfs' efforts at the Hogarth Press is not then in the merit of their printing but in the quality of their titles and the authors they published, even though some of the handprinted books raise interesting questions concerning their taste for Georgian poetry or at least, under certain circumstances, their willingness to print and publish it.

It has been suggested that the Woolfs were extremely fortunate in the authors who circulated in nearby literary orbits and who either responded favorably to invitations from the Woolfs to contribute to the Press or were sent by others aware that the author would find a sympathetic response from the Woolfs. However, many of these authors proved to be not only talented and capable of vital artistic responses to their age but were recognized as such by critics and the public rather quickly after publication. This added to the prestige of the Press and the Woolfs for having taken the chance of publishing their work. This facility for attracting talent was not merely the result of the Woolfs' availability to their talented friends in the Bloomsbury Group. They were approachable from several directions. Until the 1930s, both Woolfs wrote constantly for the reviewing journals and newspapers. These activities brought new talent to their attention. Their ties to the academic world were strong and long-lasting. Nor can we ignore the significance of the basement of Tavistock Square, where the presses and offices of the Hogarth Press were housed after 1924 and where the drop-in traffic was brisk and the turnover of young assistants kept the Woolfs abreast of current literary and social trends among England's educated middle class.

As important as anything else, and something for which the Bloomsbury Group was renowned, was conversation—the daily exchange of information and plain old gossip—which played a crucial role in people's lives before the age of mass communication, whether people walked around the square for tea or, later, telephoned. These ephemeral interchanges are only hinted at through Virginia's diaries and letters and those of others from the period but it is enough to make one envy the snail on the wall. No new light or talent with the least possibility of making a mark in the world of art, literature, music or dance was ignored by this representative crowd of interested individuals, many of whom have been introduced in the course of this study. It is impossible to recreate their exchanges now, but the knowledge that they took place, so lively at the moment, and so wonderfully contradictory with all their currents of human interaction—curiosity, jealousy, admiration, contempt—encourages us to speculate about why certain people were printed by the Woolfs and at the same time to regret our lack of certainty about so many others. Almost all the comments on publications from the Hogarth Press made by Leonard or Virginia are general or related to the technical side of getting the job done. Rarely can it be discovered what either thought about the work they printed and Virginia's comments, more often than not, reflect her state of mind rather than her critical opinion of the job she was slaving over.

By 1932 the Hogarth Press had provided the Woolfs with a distinguished list of publications and financial security. This security freed them from the task of turning out regular reviews to make ends meet and allowed them to give up activities which drained their time and energy. Mary Gaither misunderstands Leonard's initial emphasis on the Woolfs' struggle to learn printing when she comments that the Press "grew quite simply out of the Woolfs' interest in printing."[7] It was the overwhelming desire of the Woolfs to publish. When they started the Press, several friends had had major publishing triumphs. All of E.M. Forster's novels except *A Passage to India* had been published with good reviews. Clive Bell had made a startling contribution to British aesthetics with *Art* in 1914. Strachey's *Landmarks in French Literature* came out in 1912 and established him as a lively new voice, and his iconoclastic *Eminent Victorians* was about to come out in 1918. Whether the Woolfs felt a twinge of envy or not, they wanted their say too. They printed both from necessity and to have a hobby, certainly, but most of all they wanted a public for their own writings and for those of others whom they thought should have a reading. Success at the Press allowed them to give up printing but they had a difficult time relinquishing their editorial rights as publishers or giving up the Press totally. As a business and as a major contributor to twentieth-century literature, it continued on for decades after 1932, the Woolfs' symbolic power over it waning only with the publication of Leonard's last volume of autobiography, *The Journey Not the Arrival,* in

1969, the year of his death. This is a title whose meaning could summarize not only Leonard's life but also the history of his and Virginia's handprinted books.

Illustrations of the Books in Order of Publication

Figure 1.   Cover for *Two Stories* by L.S. and Virginia Woolf

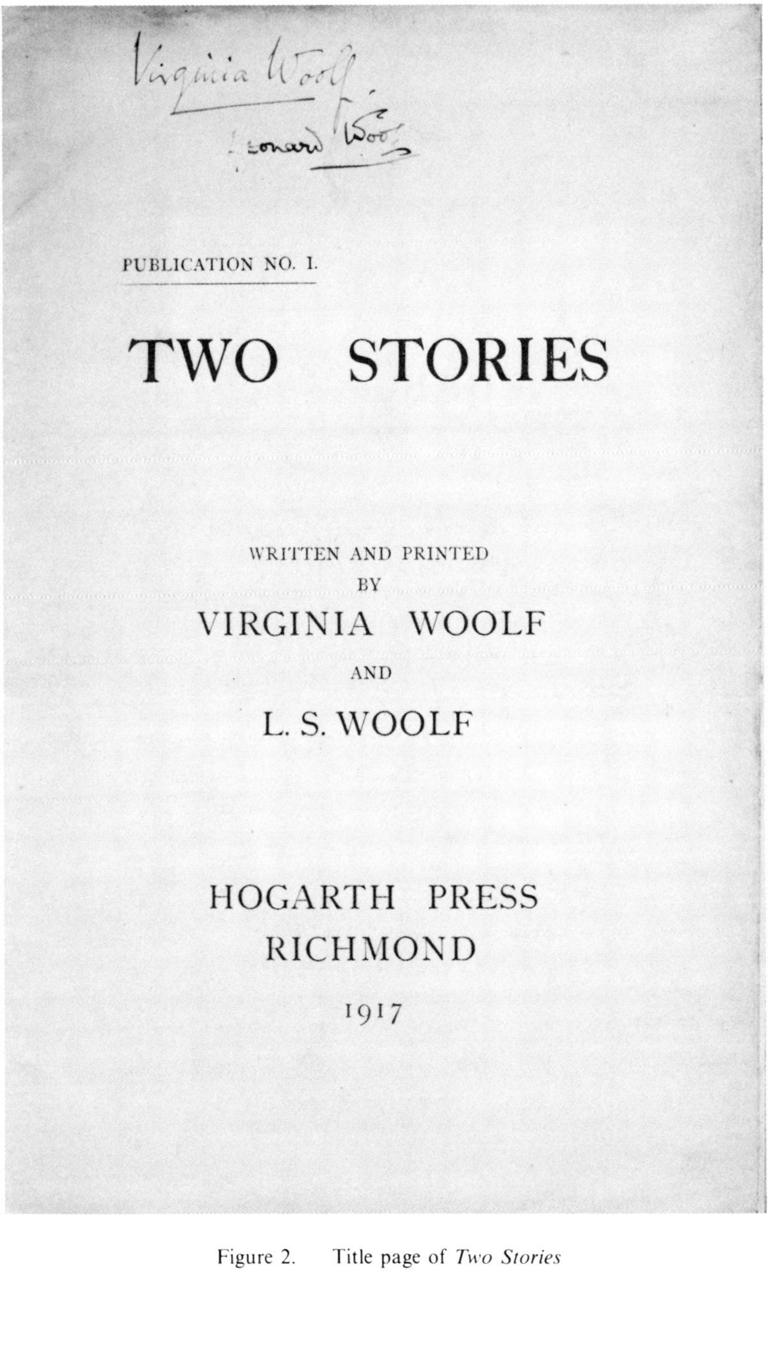

Virginia Woolf

Leonard Woolf

PUBLICATION NO. I.

TWO STORIES

WRITTEN AND PRINTED
BY
VIRGINIA WOOLF
AND
L. S. WOOLF

HOGARTH PRESS
RICHMOND

1917

Figure 2. Title page of *Two Stories*

THREE JEWS

By

LEONARD WOOLF.

It was a Sunday and the first day of spring, the first day on which one felt at any rate spring in the air. It blew in at my window with its warm breath , with its inevitable little touch of sadness . I felt restless, and I had nowhere to go to; everyone I knew was out of town. I looked out of my window at the black trees breaking into bud, the tulips and the hyacinths that even London could not rob of their reds and blues and yellows, the delicate spring sunshine on the asphalt, and the pale blue sky that the chimney pots broke into. I found myself muttering "damn it" for no very obvious reason. It was spring, I suppose, the first stirring of the blood.

I wanted to see clean trees, and the sun shine upon grass; I wanted flowers and leaves unsoiled by soot; I wanted to see and smell the earth; above all I wanted the horizon. I felt that

Figure 3.   First page of *Two Stories*

"Dad, I want to marry a girl"—a really nice girl—"but she's not one of us: will you give me your permission and blessing?" Well I don't believe in it. Our women are as good, better than Christian women. Aren't they as beautiful, as clever, as good wives? I know my poor mother, God rest her soul, used to say: "My son," she said, "if you come to me and say you want to marry a good girl, a Jewess, I don't care whether she hasn't a chemise to her back, I'll welcome her—but if you marry a Christian, if she's as rich as Solomon, I've done with you—don't you ever dare to come into my house again." Vell, I don't go as far as that, though I understand it. Times change: I might have received his wife, even though she was a Goy. But a servant girl who washed my dishes! I couldn't do it. One must have some dignity."

He stood there upright, stern, noble: a battered scarred old rock, but immovable under his seedy black coat. I couldn't offer him a shilling; I shook his hand, and left him brooding over his son and his graves.

Figure 4.   Page 18 of *Two Stories*

THE MARK ON THE WALL

By

VIRGINIA WOOLF

Perhaps it was the middle of January in the present year
that I first looked up and saw the mark on the wall. In order to
fix a date it is necessary to remember what one saw. So now I
think of the fire; the steady film of yellow light upon the page of
my book; the three chrysanthemums in the round glass bowl on
the mantelpiece. Yes, it must have been the winter time, and we
had just finished our tea, for I remember that I was smoking a
cigarette when I looked up and saw the mark on the wall for the
first time. I looked up through the smoke of my cigarette and my
eye lodged for a moment upon the burning coals, and that old
fancy of the crimson flag flapping from the castle tower came into
my mind, and I thought of the cavalcade of red knights riding up
the side of the black rock. Rather to my relief the sight of the
mark interrupted the fancy, for it is an old fancy, an automatic

Figure 5.   Title page of *The Mark on the Wall* from *Two Stories*

"Though it's no good, buying newspapers......Nothing ever happens. Curse this war! God damn this war!....All the same, I don't see why we should have a snail on our wall".

Ah, the mark on the wall! For it was a snail.

Figure 6.   Page 31 of *Two Stories*

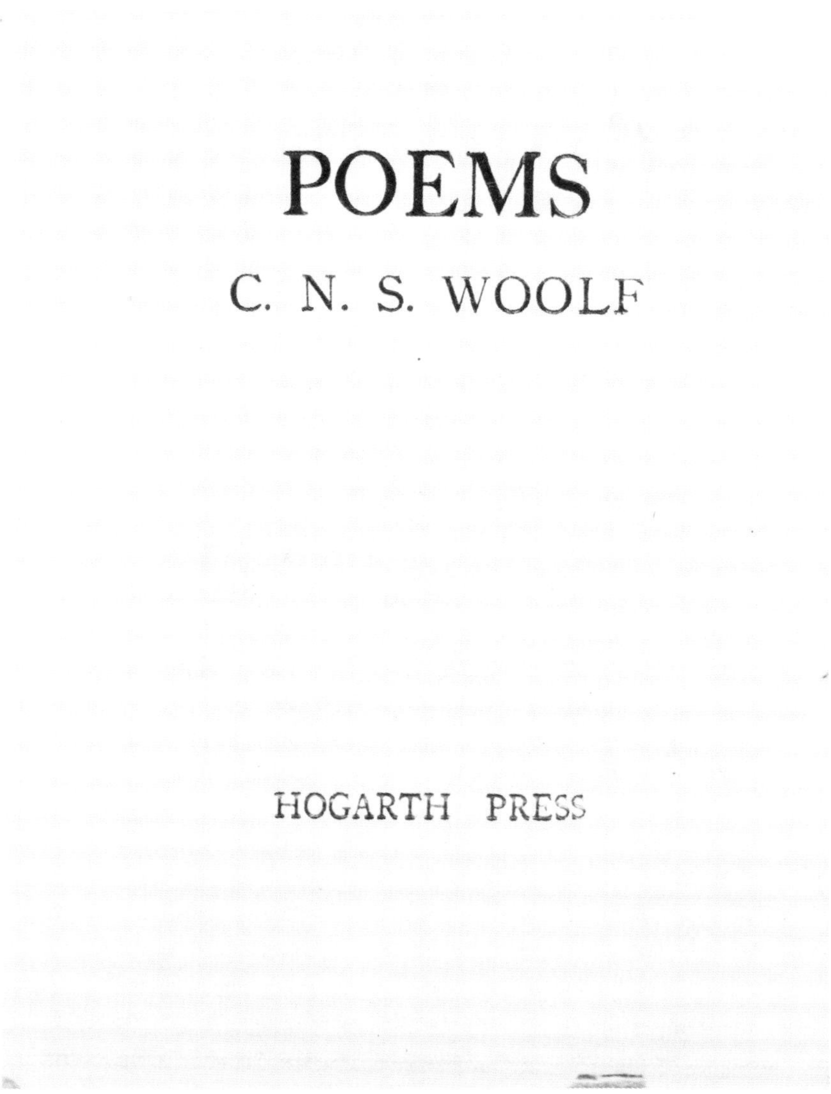

POEMS

C. N. S. WOOLF

HOGARTH PRESS

Figure 7.   Cover for *Poems* by C.N.S. Woolf

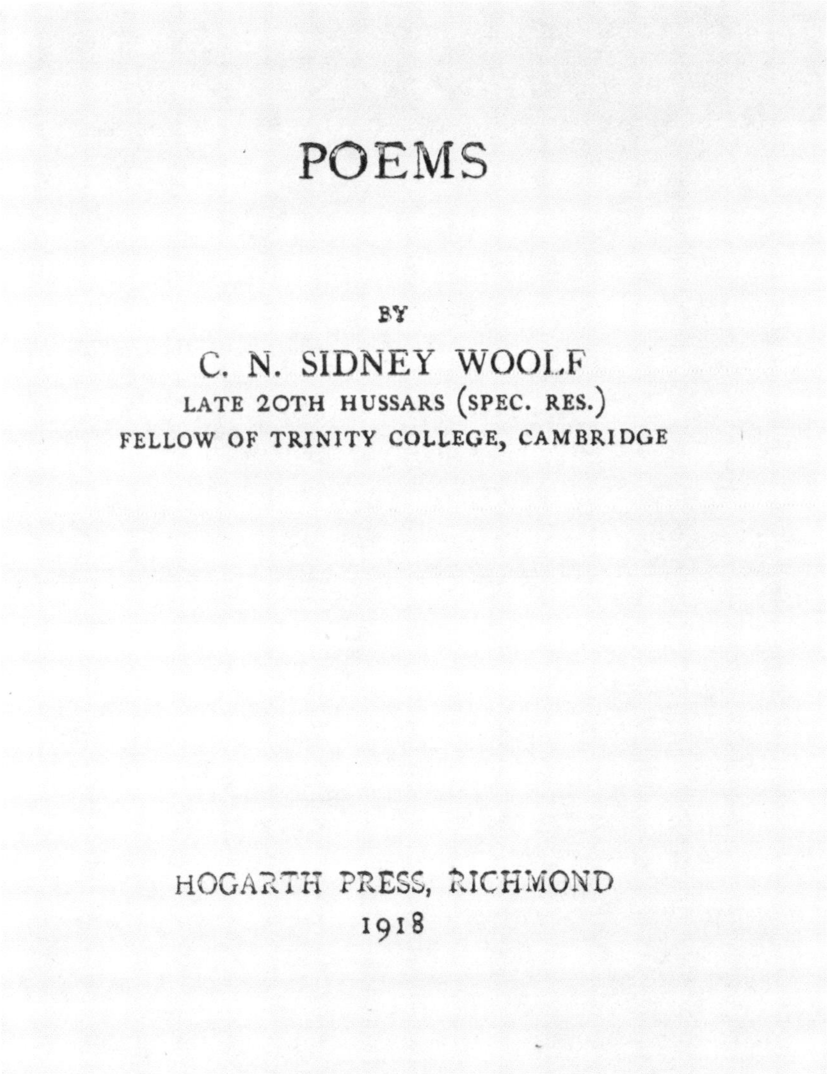

POEMS

BY

C. N. SIDNEY WOOLF

LATE 20TH HUSSARS (SPEC. RES.)
FELLOW OF TRINITY COLLEGE, CAMBRIDGE

HOGARTH PRESS, RICHMOND

1918

Figure 8. Title page of *Poems* by C.N.S. Woolf

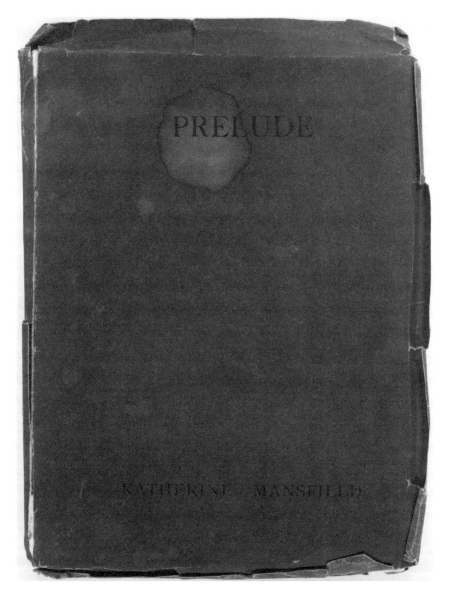

Figure 9.   Cover for *Prelude* by Katherine Mansfield

PRELUDE

BY

KATHERINE MANSFIELD

HOGARTH PRESS
RICHMOND

Figure 10. Title page of *Prelude*

Figure 11.   Cover for *Kew Gardens* by Virginia Woolf

Virginia Woolf.

KEW GARDENS

BY

VIRGINIA WOOLF

HOGARTH PRESS
RICHMOND
1919

Figure 12.   Title page of *Kew Gardens*

Figure 13.   Frontispiece for *Kew Gardens*

wavering from them as if they were flames lolling from the thick waxen bodies of candles. Voices. Yes, voices. Wordless voices, breaking the silence suddenly with such depth of contentment, such passion of desire, or, in the voices of children, such freshness of surprise; breaking the silence? But there was no silence; all the time the motor omnibuses were turning their wheels and changing their gear; like a vast nest of Chinese boxes all of wrought steel turning ceaselessly one within another the city murmured; on the top of which the voices cried aloud, and the petals of myriads of flowers flashed their colours into the air.

Printed by **L. and V. Woolf** *at The Hogarth Press, Richmond*

Figure 14.   Last page of *Kew Gardens*

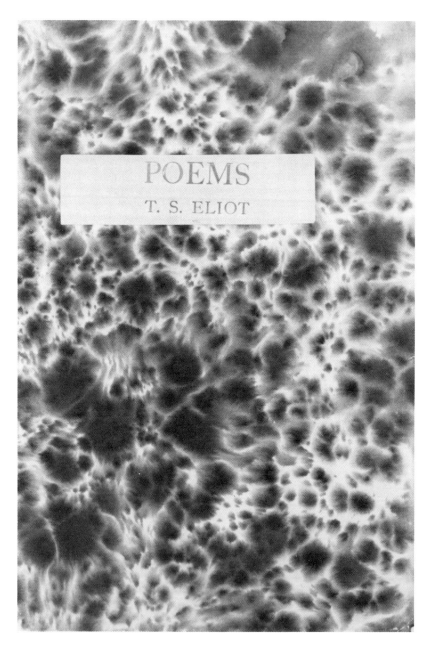

POEMS

T. S. ELIOT

Figure 15. Cover for *Poems* by T.S. Eliot

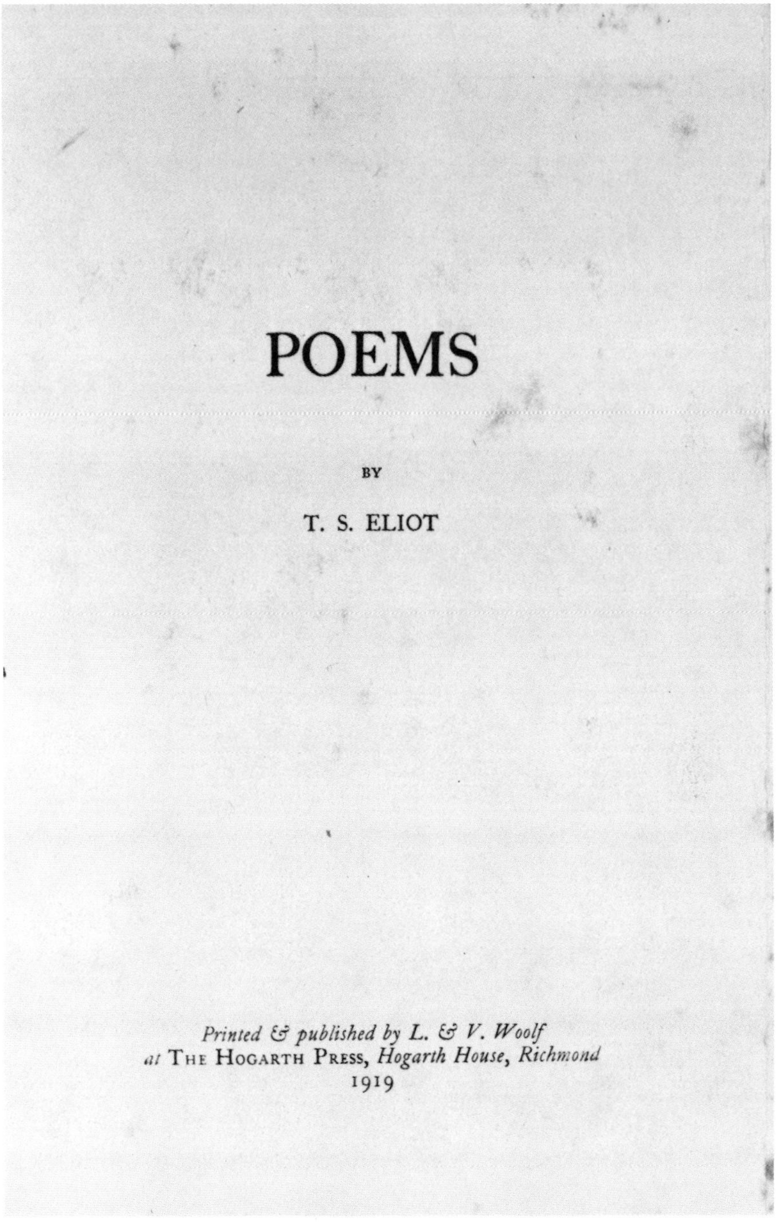

POEMS

BY

T. S. ELIOT

Printed & published by *L. & V. Woolf*
at THE HOGARTH PRESS, *Hogarth House, Richmond*
1919

Figure 16.   Title page of *Poems* by T.S. Eliot

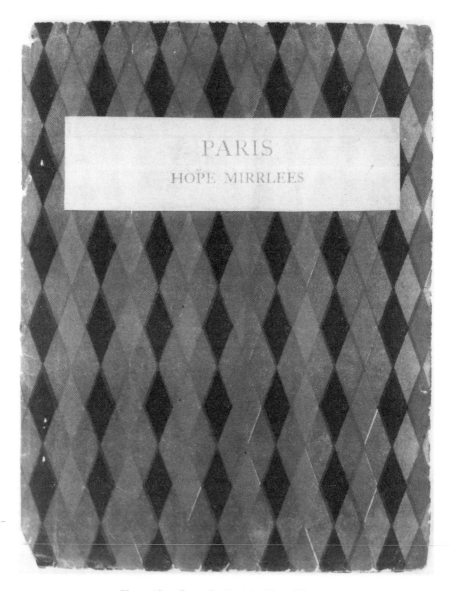

Figure 17.   Cover for *Paris* by Hope Mirrlees

PARIS

A POEM

BY

HOPE MIRRLEES

*Printed by Leonard & Virginia Woolf at
The Hogarth Press, Paradise Road, Richmond*
1919

Figure 18.   Title page of *Paris*

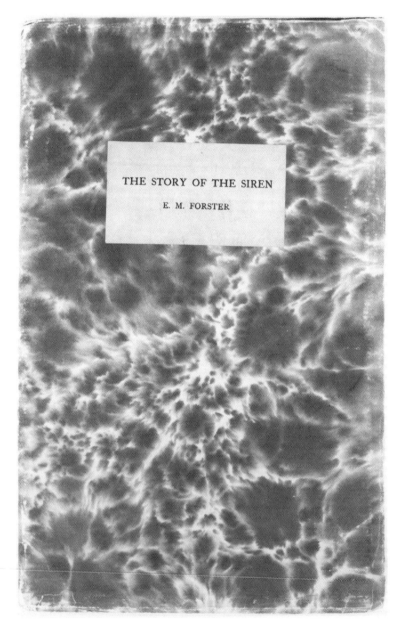

THE STORY OF THE SIREN

E. M. FORSTER

Figure 19. Cover for *The Story of the Siren* by E. M. Forster

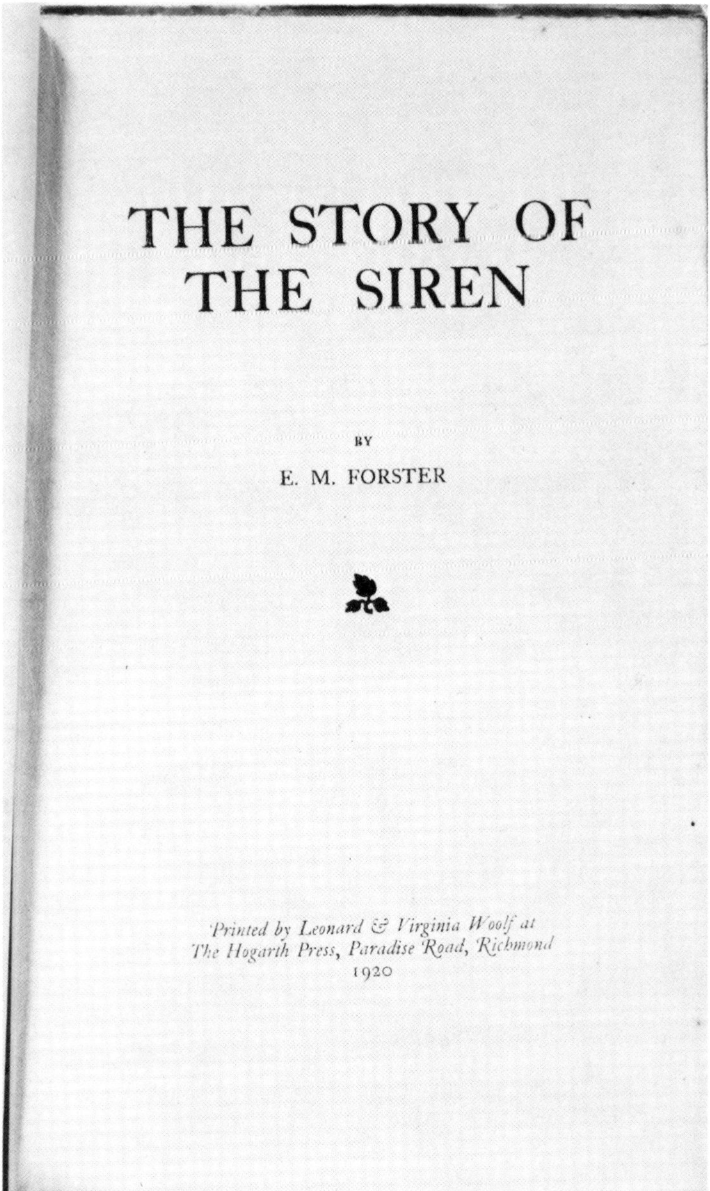

THE STORY OF
THE SIREN

BY

E. M. FORSTER

Printed by Leonard & Virginia Woolf at
The Hogarth Press, Paradise Road, Richmond
1920

Figure 20. Title page of *The Story of the Siren*

Figure 21. Cover for *Stories of the East* by Leonard Woolf

STORIES
OF THE EAST

LEONARD WOOLF

*Printed and published by Leonard and Virginia Woolf
at the Hogarth Press, Hogarth House, Richmond.*
1921

Figure 22.   Title page for *Stories of the East*

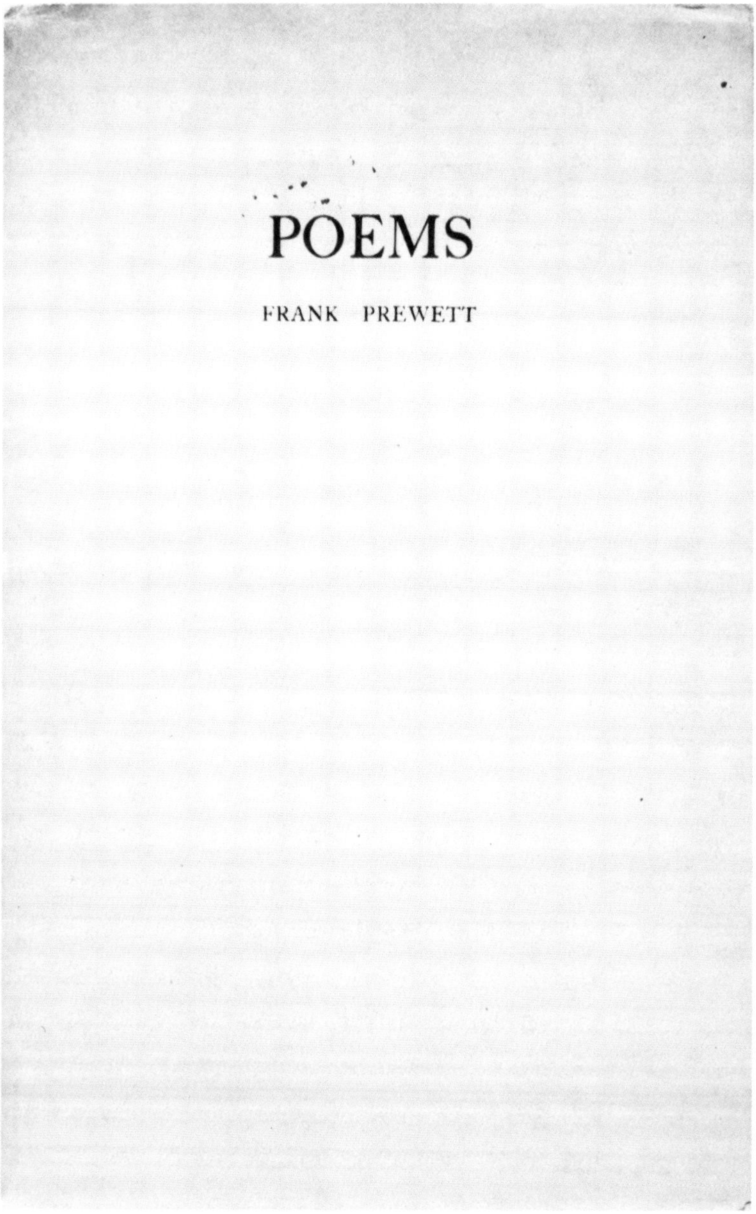

POEMS

FRANK PREWETT

Figure 23.   Cover for *Poems* by Frank Prewitt

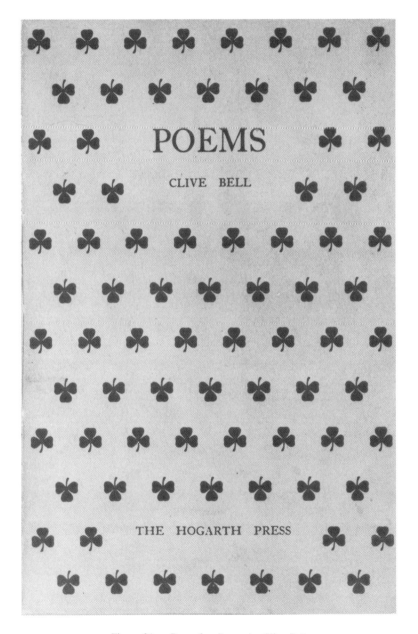

Figure 24.   Cover for *Poems* by Clive Bell

POEMS

CLIVE BELL

Printed & published by Leonard and Virginia Woolf
at the Hogarth Press, Richmond, Surrey.

1921

Figure 25.   Title page for *Poems* by Clive Bell

TWELVE ORIGINAL WOODCUTS

ROGER FRY

Figure 26.   Cover for third impression of *Twelve Original Woodcuts* by Roger Fry

TWELVE ORIGINAL WOODCUTS BY ROGER FRY

THIRD IMPRESSION

PRINTED AND PUBLISHED BY
LEONARD & VIRGINIA WOOLF
AT THE HOGARTH PRESS
HOGARTH HOUSE RICHMOND
1922

Figure 27. Title page of *Twelve Original Woodcuts*

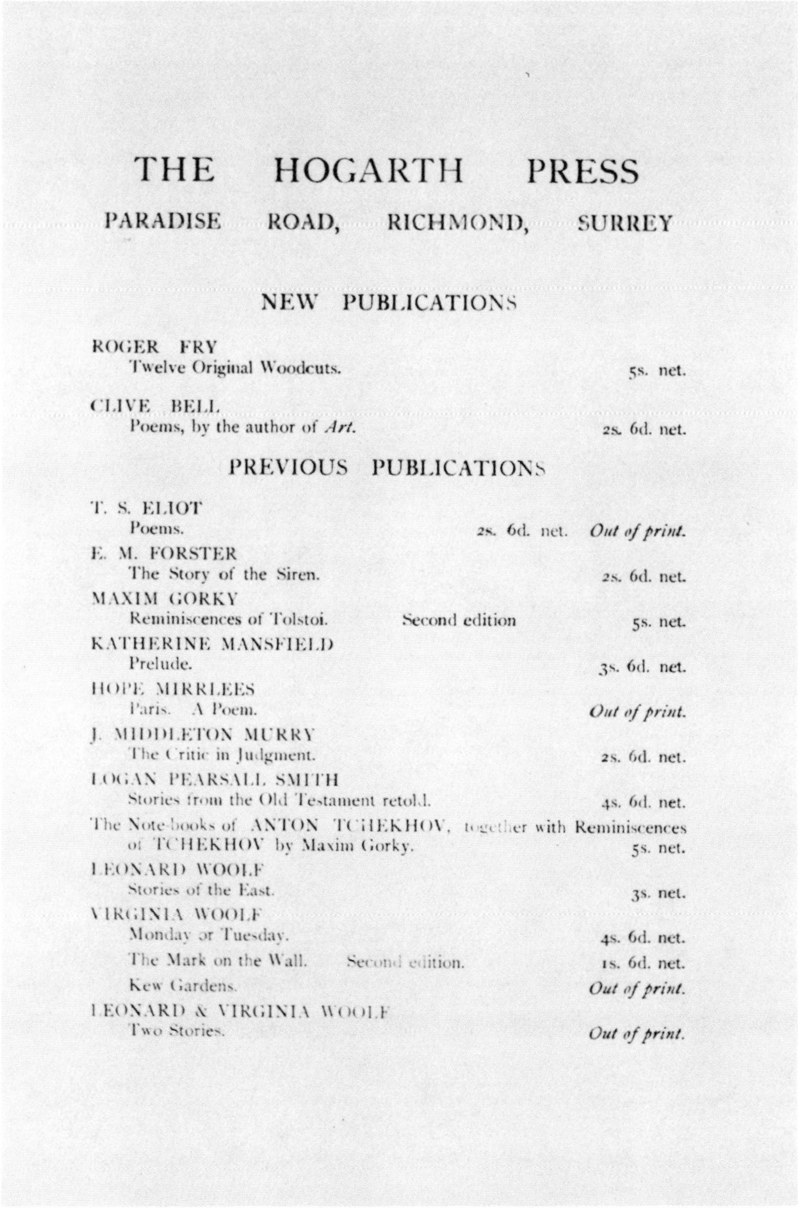

THE HOGARTH PRESS

PARADISE ROAD, RICHMOND, SURREY

NEW PUBLICATIONS

ROGER FRY
Twelve Original Woodcuts.   5s. net.

CLIVE BELL
Poems, by the author of *Art*.   2s. 6d. net.

PREVIOUS PUBLICATIONS

T. S. ELIOT
Poems.   2s. 6d. net.   *Out of print.*

E. M. FORSTER
The Story of the Siren.   2s. 6d. net.

MAXIM GORKY
Reminiscences of Tolstoi.   Second edition   5s. net.

KATHERINE MANSFIELD
Prelude.   3s. 6d. net.

HOPE MIRRLEES
Paris. A Poem.   *Out of print.*

J. MIDDLETON MURRY
The Critic in Judgment.   2s. 6d. net.

LOGAN PEARSALL SMITH
Stories from the Old Testament retold.   4s. 6d. net.

The Note-books of ANTON TCHEKHOV, together with Reminiscences
of TCHEKHOV by Maxim Gorky.   5s. net.

LEONARD WOOLF
Stories of the East.   3s. net.

VIRGINIA WOOLF
Monday or Tuesday.   4s. 6d. net.

The Mark on the Wall.   Second edition.   1s. 6d. net.

Kew Gardens.   *Out of print.*

LEONARD & VIRGINIA WOOLF
Two Stories.   *Out of print.*

Figure 28. Advertisement page from *Twelve Original Woodcuts*

Figure 29.   Cover for *Karn* by Ruth Manning-Sanders

KARN

RUTH MANNING-SANDERS

PRINTED AND PUBLISHED BY LEONARD AND VIRGINIA
WOOLF AT THE HOGARTH PRESS HOGARTH HOUSE
RICHMOND
1922

Figure 30.   Title page of *Karn*

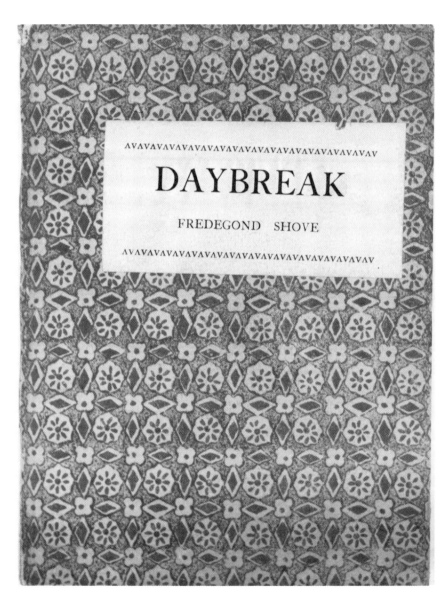

Figure 31.   Cover for *Daybreak* by Fredegond Shove

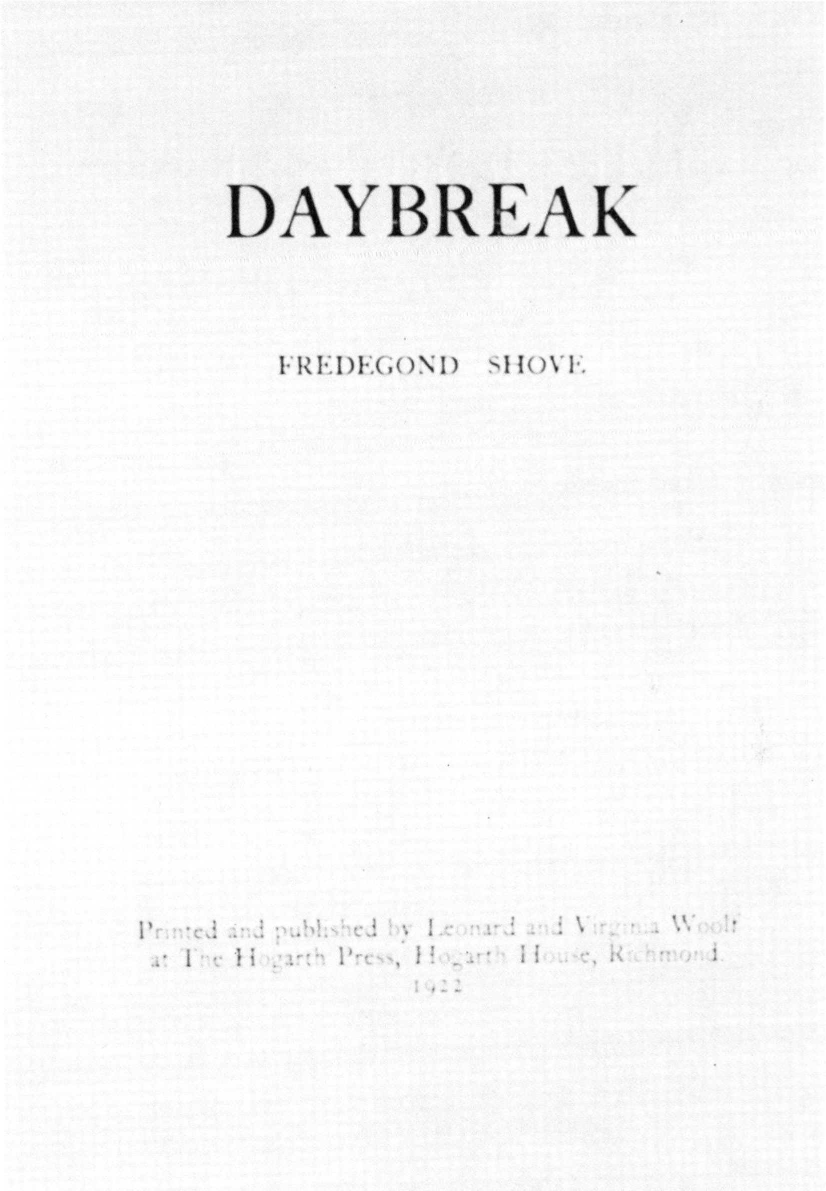

DAYBREAK

FREDEGOND SHOVE

Printed and published by Leonard and Virginia Woolf
at The Hogarth Press, Hogarth House, Richmond.
1922

Figure 32.   Title page of *Daybreak*

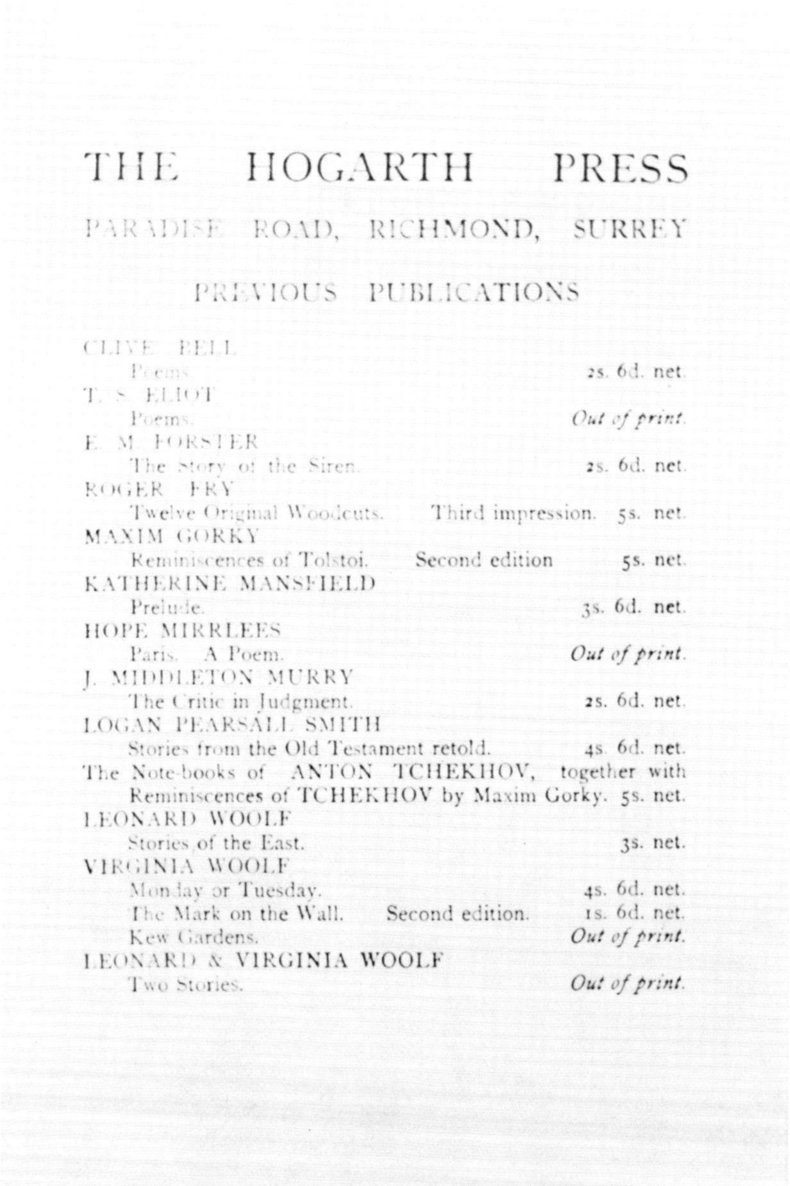

THE HOGARTH PRESS

PARADISE ROAD, RICHMOND, SURREY

PREVIOUS PUBLICATIONS

CLIVE BELL
    Poems.   2s. 6d. net.
T. S. ELIOT
    Poems.   *Out of print.*
E. M. FORSTER
    The Story of the Siren.   2s. 6d. net.
ROGER FRY
    Twelve Original Woodcuts.   Third impression.   5s. net.
MAXIM GORKY
    Reminiscences of Tolstoi.   Second edition   5s. net.
KATHERINE MANSFIELD
    Prelude.   3s. 6d. net.
HOPE MIRRLEES
    Paris. A Poem.   *Out of print.*
J. MIDDLETON MURRY
    The Critic in Judgment.   2s. 6d. net.
LOGAN PEARSALL SMITH
    Stories from the Old Testament retold.   4s. 6d. net.
The Note-books of ANTON TCHEKHOV, together with
    Reminiscences of TCHEKHOV by Maxim Gorky. 5s. net.
LEONARD WOOLF
    Stories of the East.   3s. net.
VIRGINIA WOOLF
    Monday or Tuesday.   4s. 6d. net.
    The Mark on the Wall.   Second edition.   1s. 6d. net.
    Kew Gardens.   *Out of print.*
LEONARD & VIRGINIA WOOLF
    Two Stories.   *Out of print.*

Figure 33.   Advertisement page from *Daybreak*

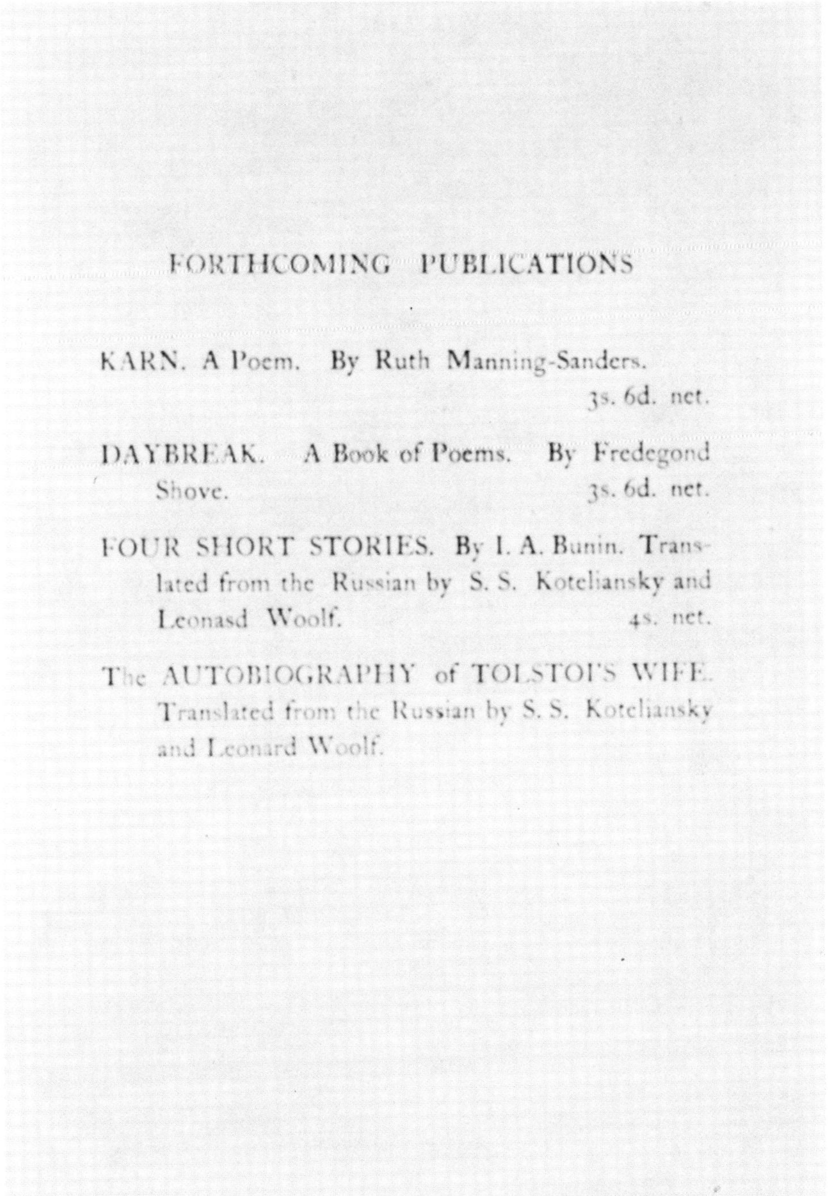

FORTHCOMING PUBLICATIONS

KARN. A Poem. By Ruth Manning-Sanders.
3s. 6d. net.

DAYBREAK. A Book of Poems. By Fredegond
Shove. 3s. 6d. net.

FOUR SHORT STORIES. By I. A. Bunin. Translated from the Russian by S. S. Koteliansky and
Leonasd Woolf. 4s. net.

The AUTOBIOGRAPHY of TOLSTOI'S WIFE.
Translated from the Russian by S. S. Koteliansky
and Leonard Woolf.

Figure 34. Advertisement page from *Daybreak*

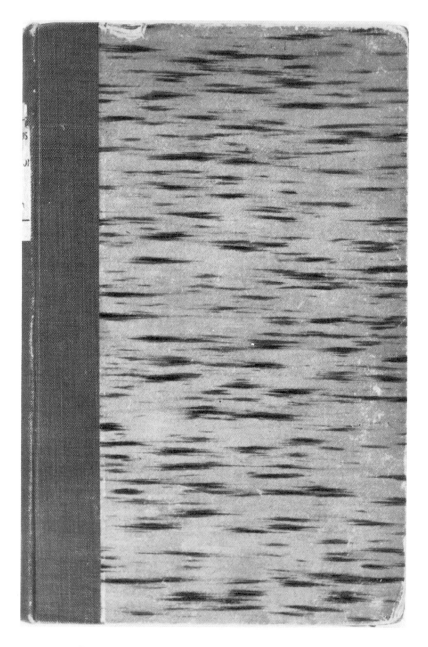

Figure 35.   Cover for *Pharos and Pharillon* by E. M. Forster

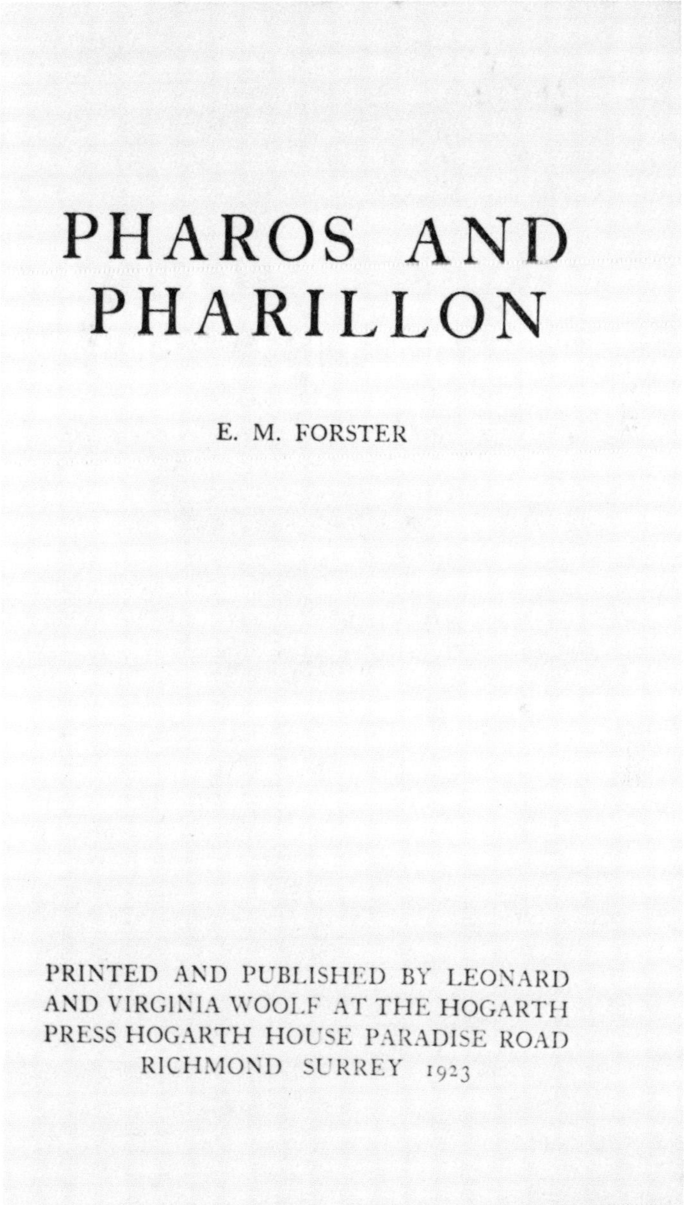

PHAROS AND PHARILLON

E. M. FORSTER

PRINTED AND PUBLISHED BY LEONARD
AND VIRGINIA WOOLF AT THE HOGARTH
PRESS HOGARTH HOUSE PARADISE ROAD
RICHMOND SURREY 1923

Figure 36.   Title page of *Pharos and Pharillon*

BY THE SAME AUTHOR

———

ALEXANDRIA : A HISTORY AND GUIDE

AGENTS, MESSRS. WHITEHEAD MORRIS
9 FENCHURCH STREET E. C.

———

THE STORY OF THE SIREN

HOGARTH PRESS

———

HOWARD'S END

EDWARD ARNOLD

Figure 37.   List of books by the author of *Pharos and Pharillon*

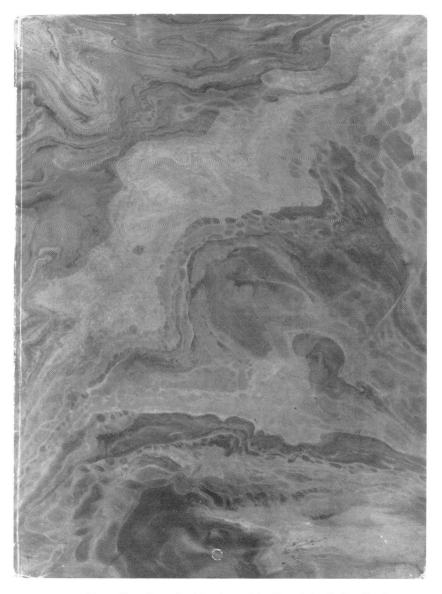

Figure 38.   Cover for *Mutations of the Phoenix* by Herbert Read

MUTATIONS OF
THE PHŒNIX

HERBERT READ

PRINTED   AND   PUBLISHED   BY
LEONARD   &   VIRGINIA   WOOLF
AT   THE   HOGARTH   PRESS
HOGARTH   HOUSE   RICHMOND
1923

Figure 39.   Title page of *Mutations of the Phoenix*

Figure 40.   Cover for *The Feather Bed* by Robert Graves

THE FEATHER BED
BY ROBERT GRAVES

With a cover design by WILLIAM NICHOLSON

PRINTED AND PUBLISHED BY
LEONARD & VIRGINIA WOOLF
AT THE HOGARTH PRESS
HOGARTH HOUSE RICHMOND
1923

Figure 41.   Title page of *The Feather Bed*

TO A PROUD PHANTOM
ENA LIMEBEER

Figure 42.   Cover for *To a Proud Phantom* by Ena Limebeer

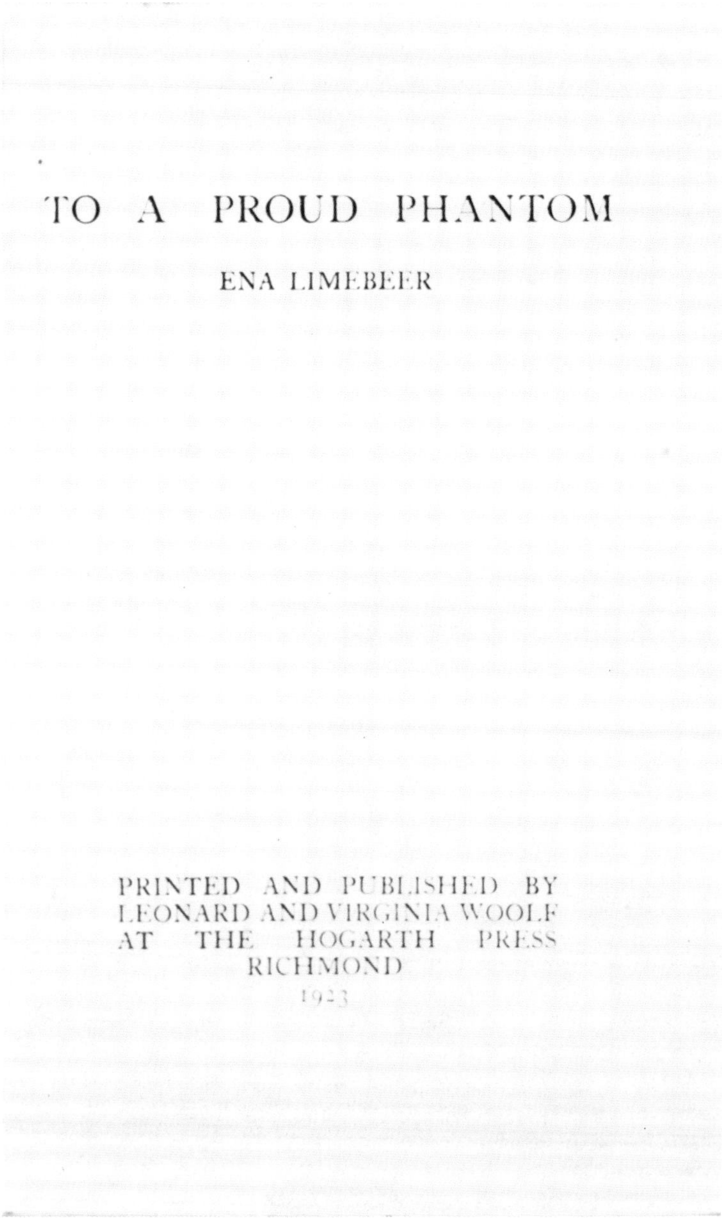

TO A PROUD PHANTOM

ENA LIMEBEER

PRINTED AND PUBLISHED BY
LEONARD AND VIRGINIA WOOLF
AT THE HOGARTH PRESS
RICHMOND
1923

Figure 43. Title page of *To a Proud Phantom*

Figure 44. Cover for *The Waste Land* by T.S. Eliot

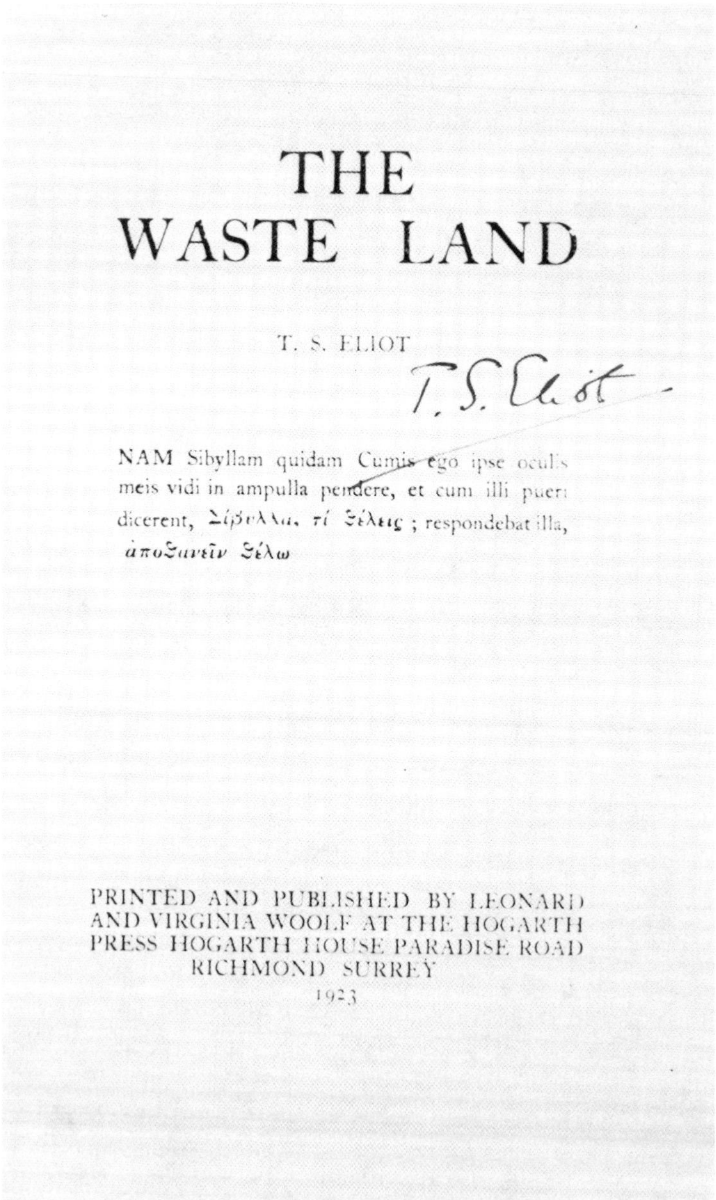

THE
WASTE LAND

T. S. ELIOT

T. S. Eliot

NAM Sibyllam quidam Cumis ego ipse oculis
meis vidi in ampulla pendere, et cum illi pueri
dicerent, Σίβυλλα, τί θέλεις ; respondebat illa,
ἀποθανεῖν θέλω

PRINTED AND PUBLISHED BY LEONARD
AND VIRGINIA WOOLF AT THE HOGARTH
PRESS HOGARTH HOUSE PARADISE ROAD
RICHMOND SURREY
1923

Figure 45. Title page of *The Waste Land*

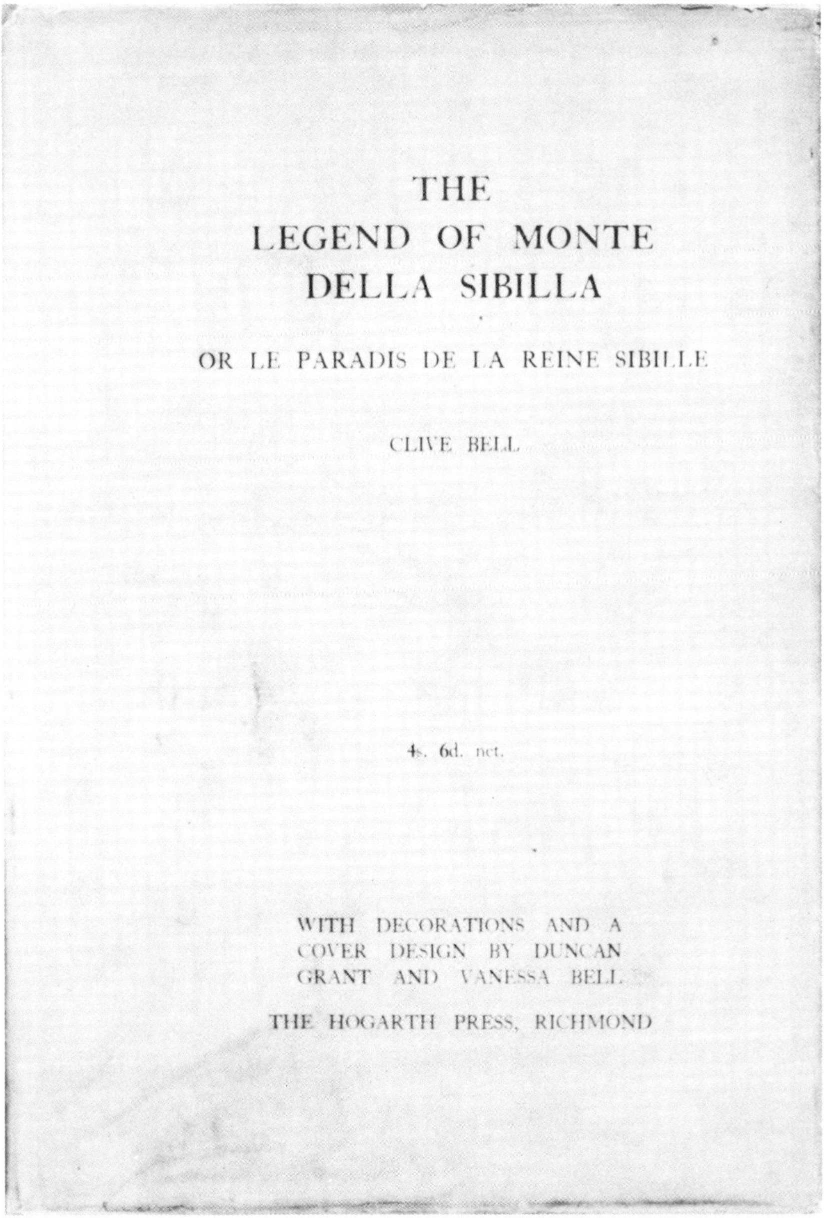

THE
LEGEND OF MONTE
DELLA SIBILLA

OR LE PARADIS DE LA REINE SIBILLE

CLIVE BELL

4s. 6d. net.

WITH DECORATIONS AND A
COVER DESIGN BY DUNCAN
GRANT AND VANESSA BELL

THE HOGARTH PRESS, RICHMOND

Figure 46.   Dust jacket for *The Legend of Monte Della Sibilla* by Clive Bell

Figure 47.   Cover for *The Legend of Monte Della Sibilla*

THE
LEGEND OF MONTE
DELLA SIBILLA
OR LE PARADIS DE LA REINE SIBILLE

CLIVE BELL

PRINTED AND PUBLISHED BY
LEONARD AND VIRGINIA WOOLF
AT THE HOGARTH PRESS
HOGARTH HOUSE RICHMOND
1923

Figure 48.   Title page of *The Legend of Monte Della Sibilla*

Figure 49.   Frontispiece for *The Legend of Monte Della Sibilla*

If you will stop and take a drink
Where I did, late one afternoon
In April, you may see turn pink
A patch of snow, which very soon
Yellows to green: it seems quite near;
But is, in fact, up Norcia way
Or further: the effect's more queer
Than beautiful: and should you say
To the *padrone*, Gian Mannino,
"What peak is that which looks so odd?"
He'll answer, "Monte Sibillino—
But they've bunged up the hole, thank God."

Figure 50.   First page of *The Legend of Monte Della Sibilla*

May hold that there is more to do
Than laugh and let the world go by
Saying "To-morrow we shall die";
Yet in a matter so obscure
Wise men may differ to be sure.
Myself, I never thought it clever
To fuss about the "grand forever",
And cultivate a soul with care for
That vast but vague hereafter ; wherefore
In my opinion, you did well
To live for love, though love is hell.

Figure 51.   Last page of *The Legend of Monte Della Sibilla*

Figure 52.   Cover for *Henry James at Work* by Theodora Bosanquet

Henry James at Work

by

Theodora Bosanquet

Printed and published by Leonard and Virginia Woolf
at The Hogarth Press, 52 Tavistock Square, London.
1924

Figure 53.   Title page of *Henry James at Work*

GRACE AFTER MEAT

JOHN CROWE RANSOM

Figure 54.   Cover for *Grace after Meat* by John Crowe Ransom

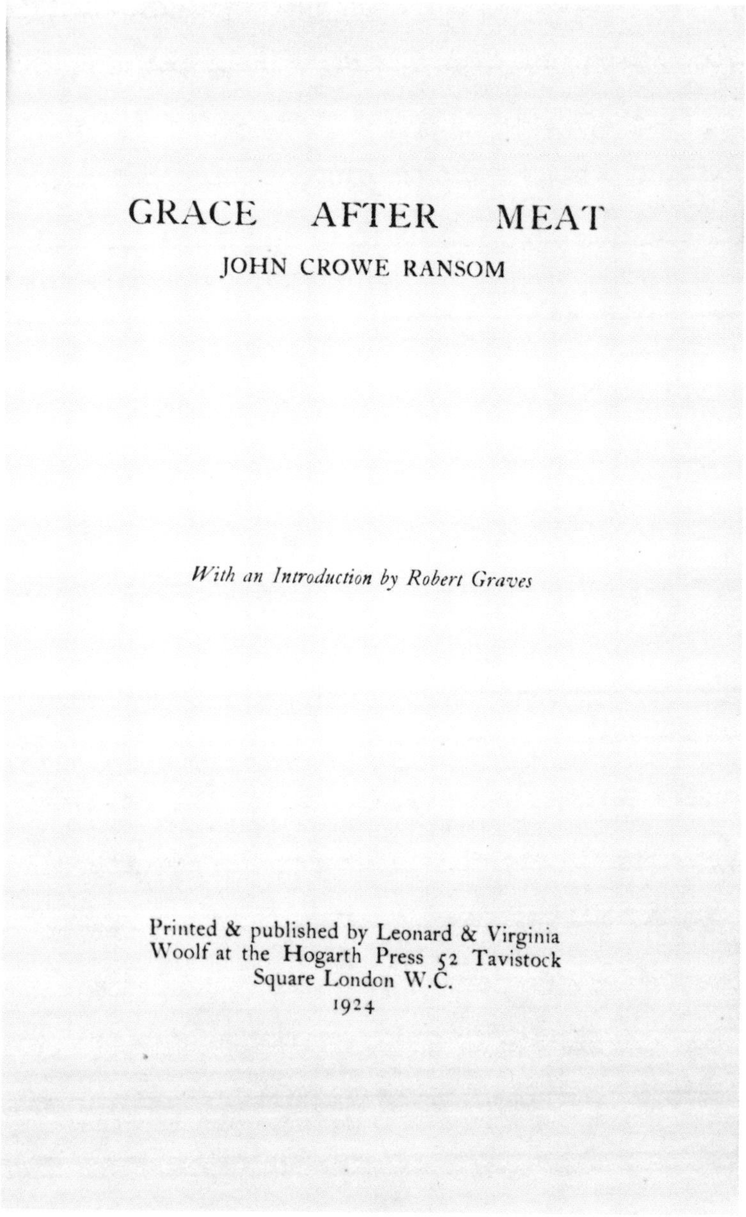

GRACE AFTER MEAT

JOHN CROWE RANSOM

With an Introduction by Robert Graves

Printed & published by Leonard & Virginia
Woolf at the Hogarth Press 52 Tavistock
Square London W.C.
1924

Figure 55.   Title page for *Grace after Meat*

Figure 56.   Cover for *Parallax* by Nancy Cunard

Figure 57.   Back for *Parallax*

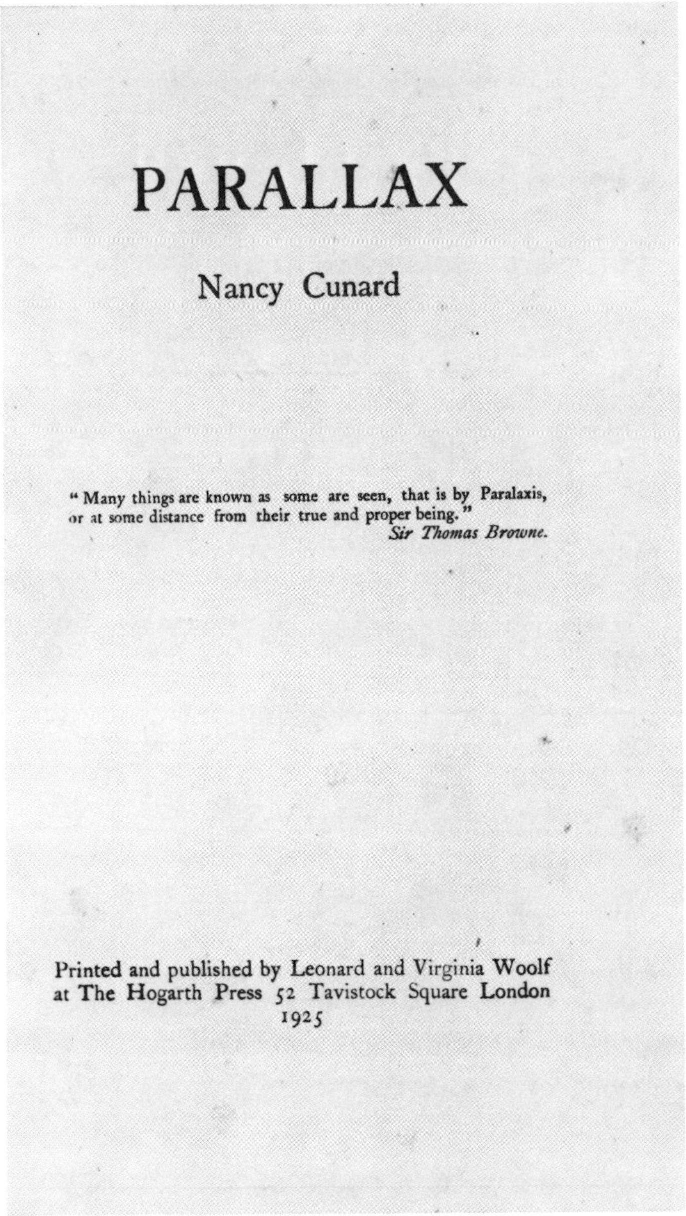

PARALLAX

Nancy Cunard

"Many things are known as some are seen, that is by Paralaxis,
or at some distance from their true and proper being."

Sir Thomas Browne.

Printed and published by Leonard and Virginia Woolf
at The Hogarth Press 52 Tavistock Square London
1925

Figure 58.   Title page of *Parallax*

POEMS AND FABLES

R. C. TREVELYAN

Figure 59. Cover for *Poems and Fables* by R.C. Trevelyan

POEMS AND FABLES

R. C. TREVELYAN

Printed and published by Leonard and Virginia
Woolf at 52 Tavistock Square London W.C.
1925

Figure 60.   Title page of *Poems and Fables*

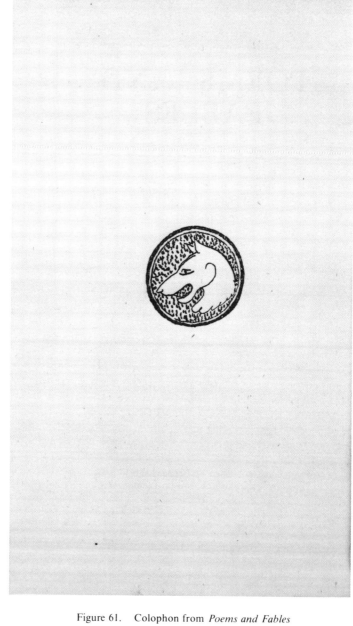

Figure 61.   Colophon from *Poems and Fables*

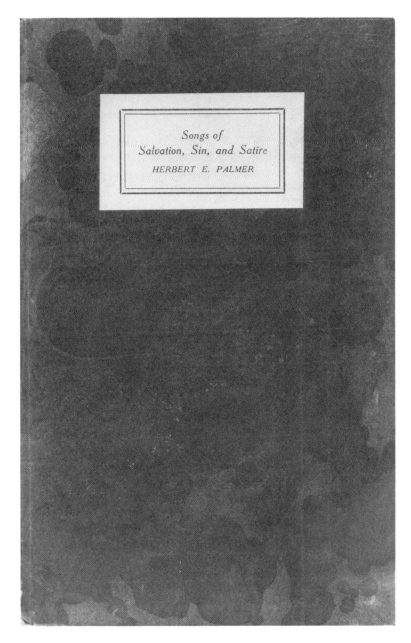

Figure 62.   Cover for *Songs of Salvation, Sin and Satire* by Herbert E. Palmer

Songs of
Salvation Sin & Satire

HERBERT E. PALMER

Printed & published by Leonard & Virginia Woolf
at The Hogarth Press, 52 Tavistock Square, London, W.C.

Figure 63.   Title page of *Songs of Salvation, Sin and Satire*

Figure 64.   Cover for *Russet and Taffeta* by George Rylands

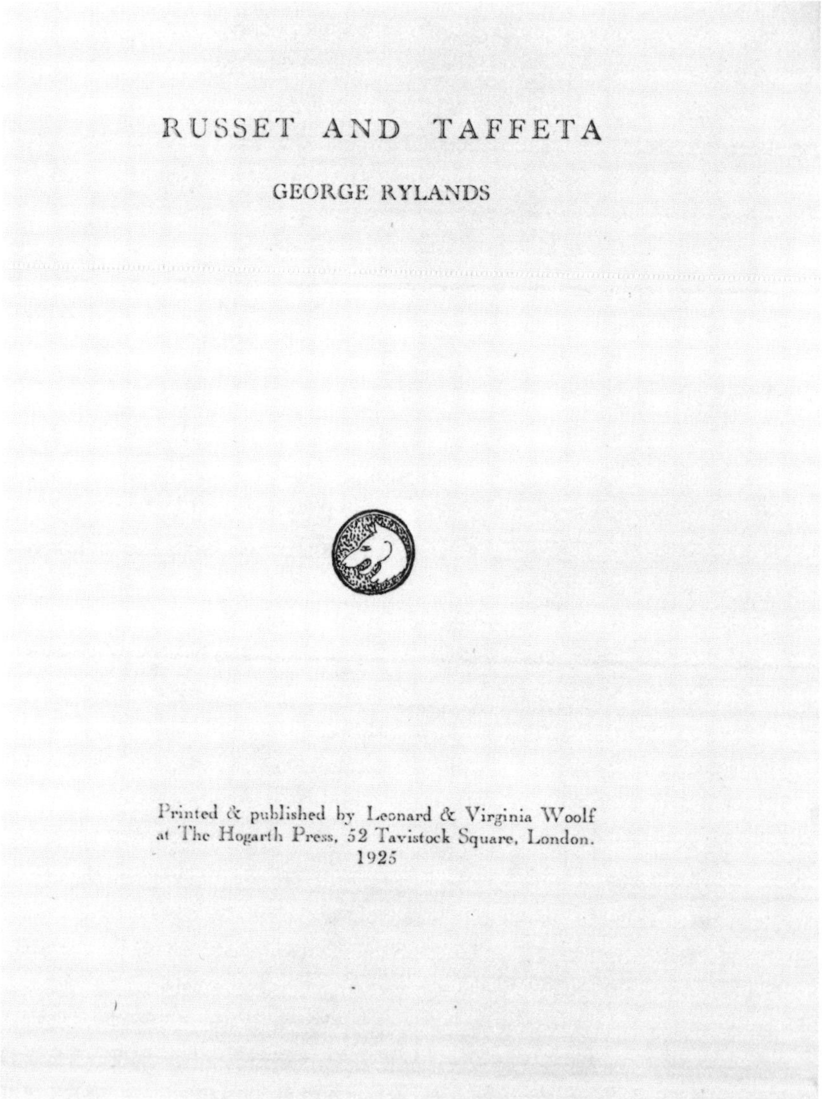

RUSSET AND TAFFETA

GEORGE RYLANDS

Printed & published by Leonard & Virginia Woolf
at The Hogarth Press, 52 Tavistock Square, London.
1925

Figure 65.   Title page of *Russet and Taffeta*

Figure 66.   Cover for *Martha-Wish-You-Ill* by Ruth Manning-Sanders

MARTHA WISH-YOU-ILL

RUTH MANNING-SANDERS

Printed & published by Leonard & Virginia
Woolf at The Hogarth Press, London. 1926.

Figure 67.   Title page for *Martha-Wish-You-Ill*

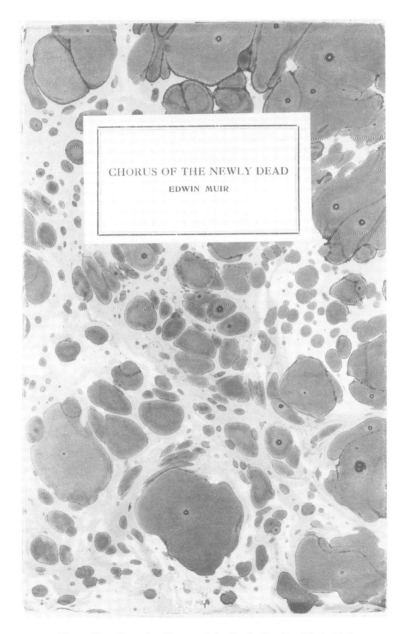

Figure 68.   Cover for *Chorus of the Newly Dead* by Edwin Muir

CHORUS OF THE NEWLY
DEAD

EDWIN MUIR

Printed & published by Leonard & Virginia
Woolf at The Hogarth Press, London. 1926.

Figure 69.   Title page of *Chorus of the Newly Dead*

APRIL MORNING

STANLEY SNAITH

Figure 70.   Cover for *April Morning* by Stanley Snaith

APRIL MORNING

STANLEY SNAITH

Printed & published by Leonard & Virginia
Woolf at The Hogarth Press, London. 1926.

Figure 71.   Title page of *April Morning*

Figure 72.   Cover for *Voltaire* by Laura Riding

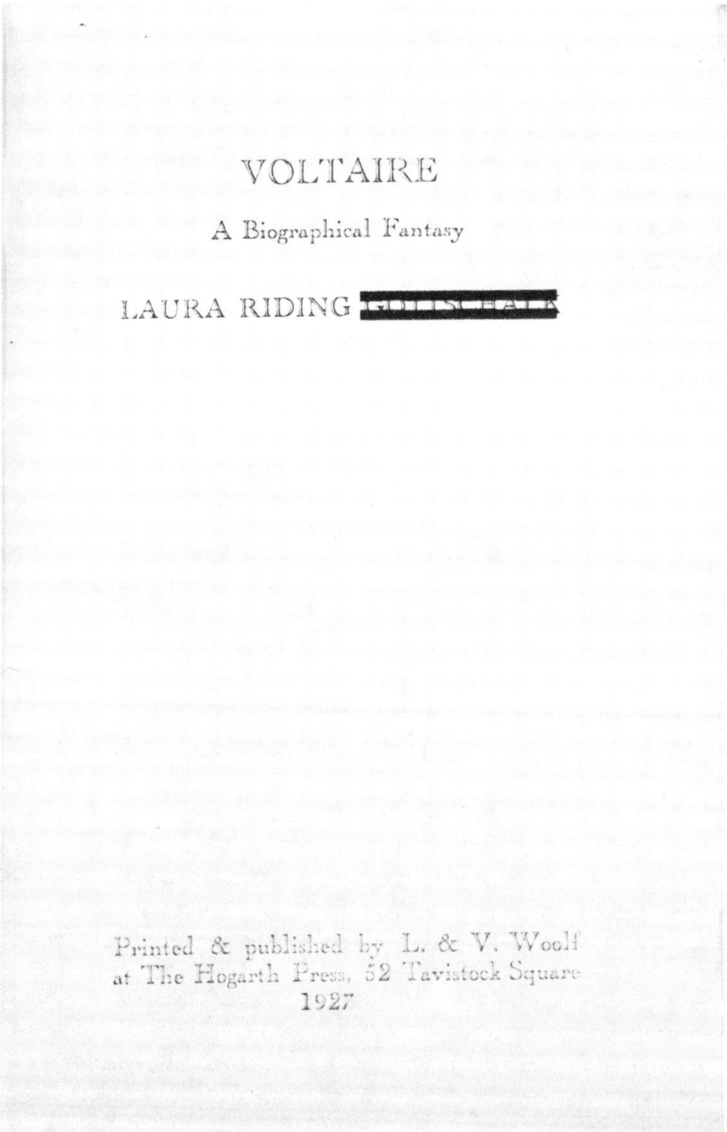

VOLTAIRE

A Biographical Fantasy

LAURA RIDING ▬▬▬▬▬▬▬

Printed & published by L. & V. Woolf
at The Hogarth Press, 52 Tavistock Square
1927

Figure 73.   Title page of *Voltaire*

VOLTAIRE .

Figure 74.   Frontispiece for *Voltaire*

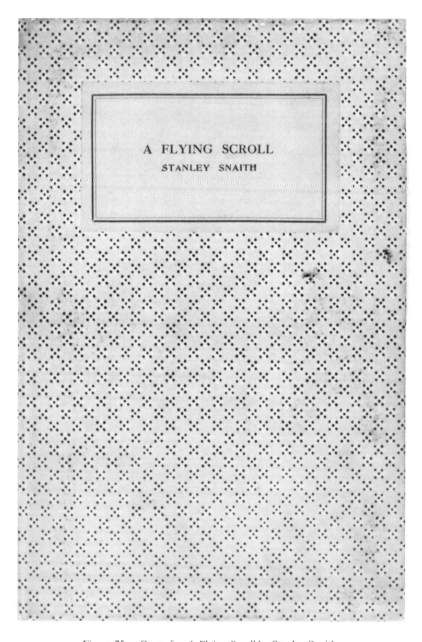

Figure 75.   Cover for *A Flying Scroll* by Stanley Snaith

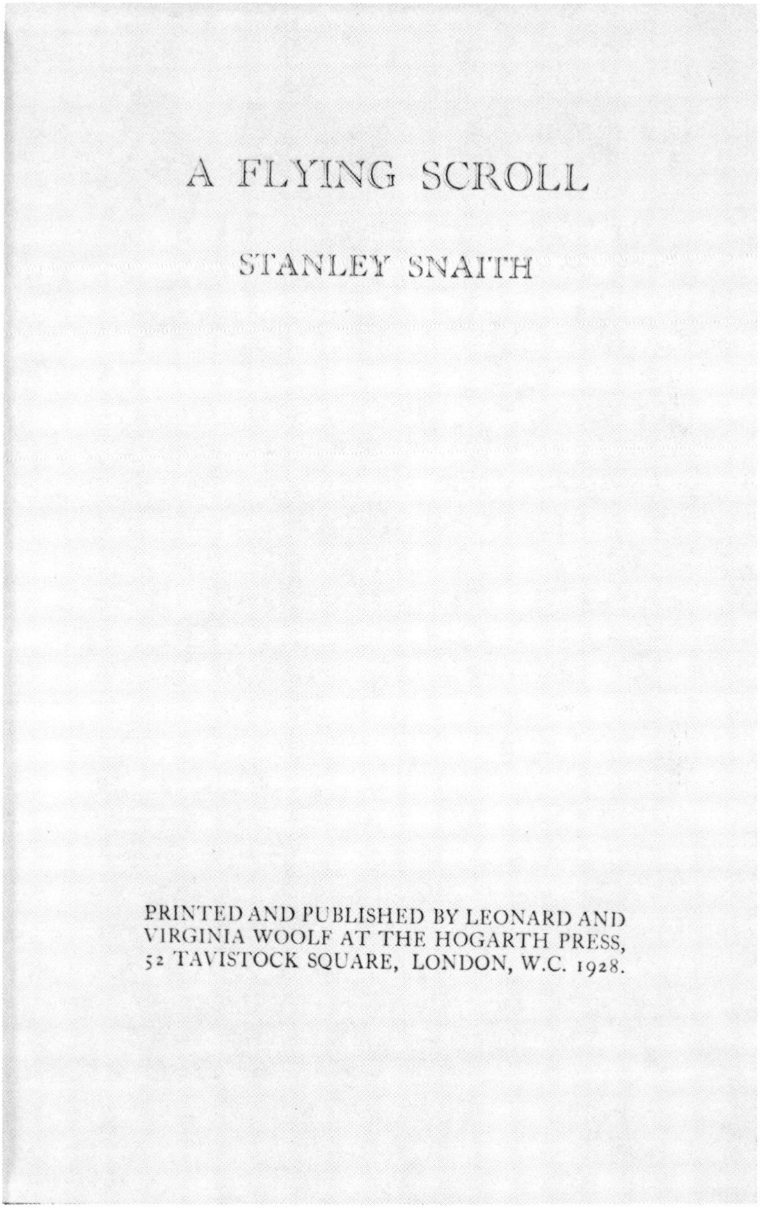

A FLYING SCROLL

STANLEY SNAITH

PRINTED AND PUBLISHED BY LEONARD AND
VIRGINIA WOOLF AT THE HOGARTH PRESS,
52 TAVISTOCK SQUARE, LONDON, W.C. 1928.

Figure 76.   Title page of *A Flying Scroll*

Figure 77.   Cover for *On Being Ill* by Virginia Woolf

Figure 78.   Back of *On Being Ill*

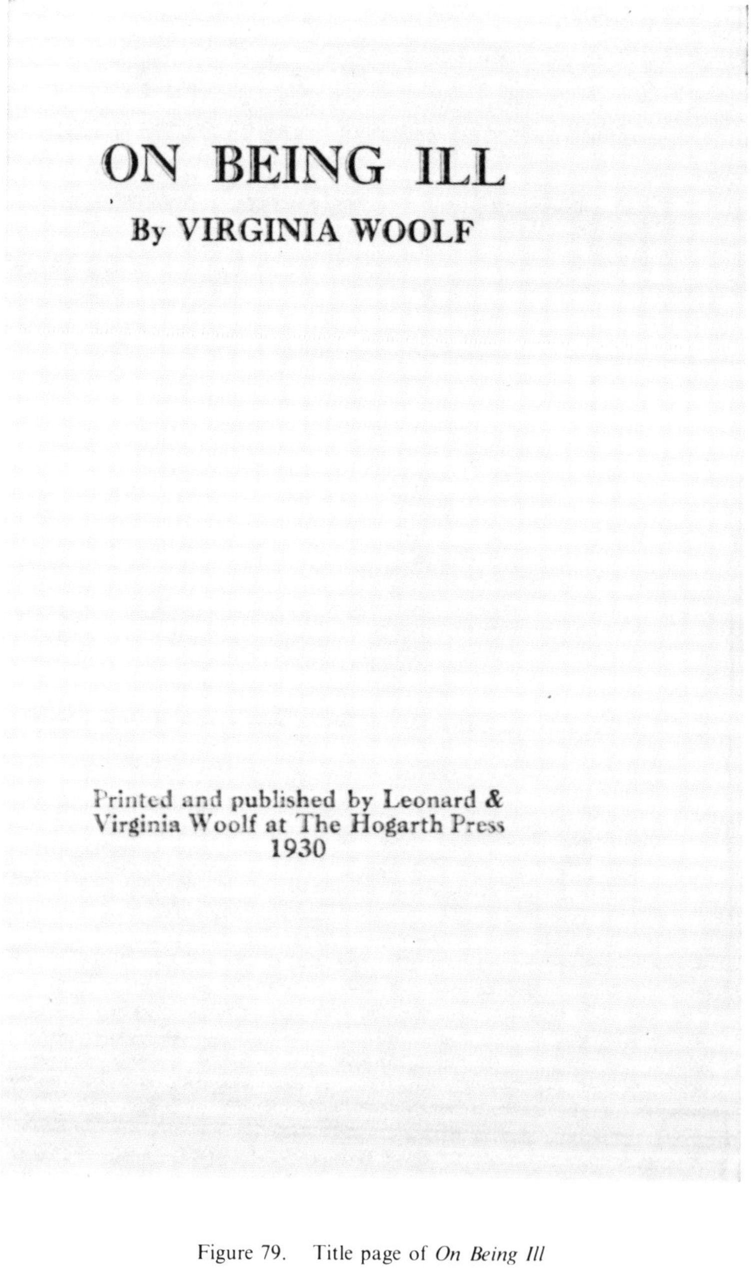

ON BEING ILL

By VIRGINIA WOOLF

Printed and published by Leonard &
Virginia Woolf at The Hogarth Press
1930

Figure 79.   Title page of *On Being Ill*

SISSINGHURST

V. SACKVILLE-WEST

THE HOGARTH PRESS

Figure 80.   Cover for *Sissinghurst* by V. Sackville-West

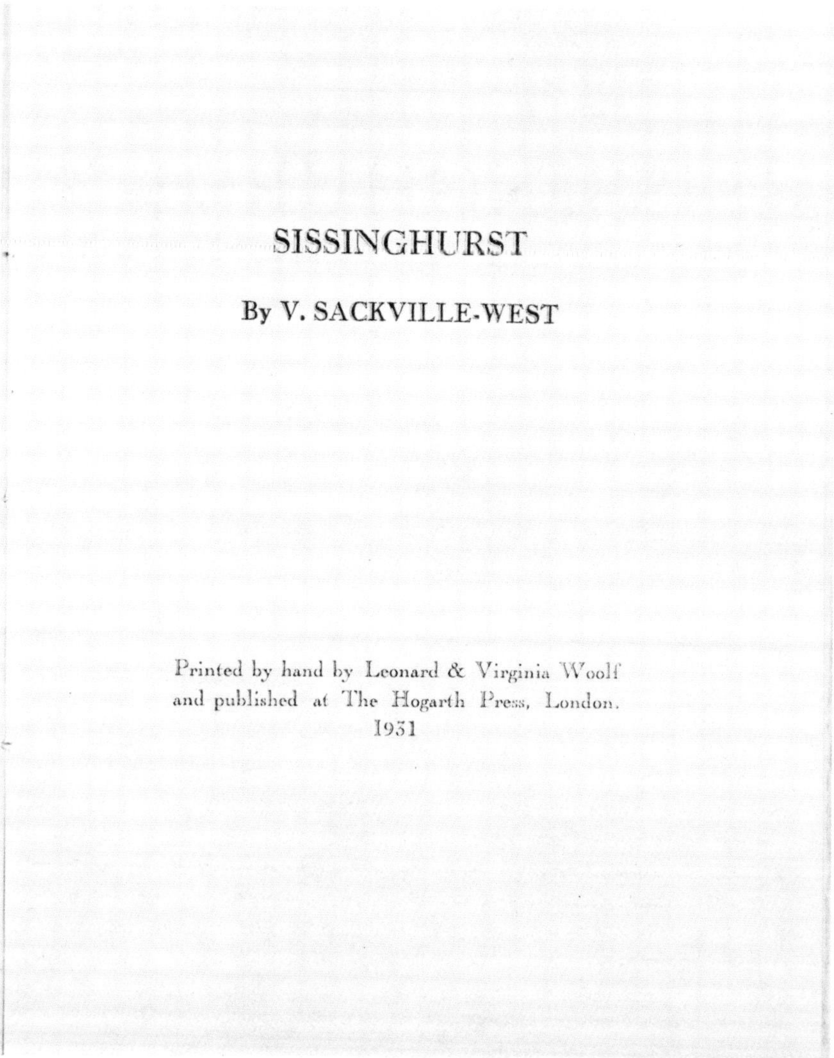

SISSINGHURST

By V. SACKVILLE-WEST

Printed by hand by Leonard & Virginia Woolf
and published at The Hogarth Press, London.
1931

Figure 81.   Title page of *Sissinghurst*

Sissinghurst,
Thursday. To V. W.

A TIRED swimmer in the waves of time
I throw my hands up : let the surface close :
Sink down through centuries to another clime,
And buried find the castle and the rose.
Buried in time and sleep,
So drowsy, overgrown,
That here the moss is green upon the stone,
And lichen stains the keep.
I've sunk into an image, water-drowned,
Where stirs no wind and penetrates no sound,
Illusive, fragile to a touch, remote,
Foundered within the well of years as deep
As in the waters of a stagnant moat.
Yet in and out of these decaying halls
I move, and not a ripple, not a quiver,
Shakes the reflection though the waters shiver,—
My tread is to the same illusion bound.
Here, tall and damask as a summer flower,

Figure 82. First page of *Sissinghurst*

Figure 83.   Cover for *Poems* by George Rylands

POEMS

By GEORGE RYLANDS

houres, dayes, moneths, which are the rags of time.
Donne.

Printed & published by L, & V. Woolf
at The Hogarth Press, London. 1931.

Figure 84.   Title page of *Poems* by George Rylands

Figure 85. Cover for *Jupiter and the Nun* by Dorothy Wellesley

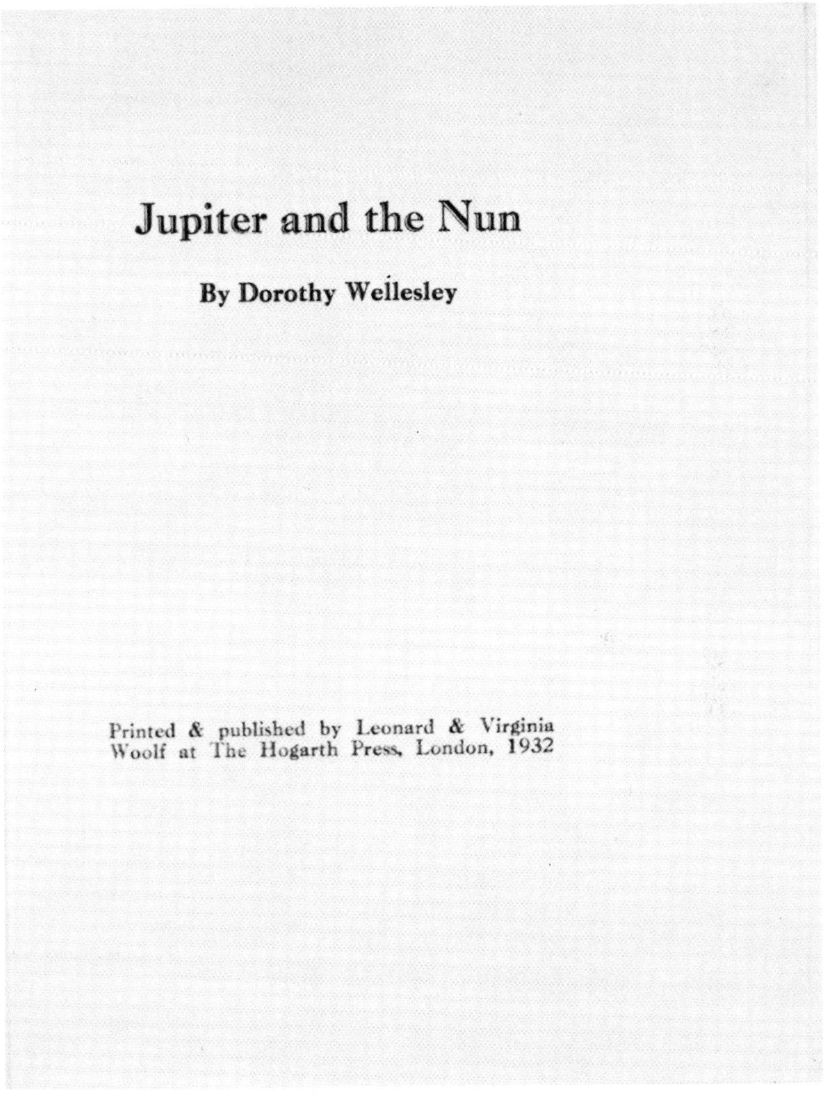

Jupiter and the Nun

By Dorothy Wellesley

Printed & published by Leonard & Virginia
Woolf at The Hogarth Press, London, 1932

Figure 86. Title page of *Jupiter and the Nun*

Appendix A

List of Handprinted Books in Order of Publication

1917	July	L. S. and Virginia Woolf, *Two Stories*
1918	March?	C. N. Sidney Woolf, *Poems*
	May	Katherine Mansfield, *Prelude*
1919	May	T. S. Eliot, *Poems*
	May	Virginia Woolf, *Kew Gardens*
1920	May	Hope Mirrlees, *Paris*
	July	E. M. Forster, *The Story of the Siren*
1921	April	Leonard Woolf, *Stories of the East*
	August	Frank Prewitt, *Poems*
	December	Clive Bell, *Poems*
	December	Roger Fry, *Twelve Original Woodcuts*
1922	May	Ruth Manning-Sanders, *Karn*
	May	Fredegond Shove, *Daybreak*
1923	May	E. M. Forster, *Pharos and Pharillon*
	May	Herbert Read, *Mutations of the Phoenix*
	July	Robert Graves, *The Feather Bed*
	July?	Ena Limebeer, *To a Proud Phantom*
	September	T. S. Eliot, *The Waste Land*
	December	Clive Bell, *The Legend of Monte Della Sibilla*
1924	May	John Crow Ransom, *Grace after Meat*
	November	Theodora Bosanquet, *Henry James at Work*
1925	April	Nancy Cunard, *Parallax*
	April	R. C. Trevelyan, *Poems and Fables*
	October	Herbert E. Palmer, *Songs of Salvation, Sin, and Satire*
	December	George Rylands, *Russet and Taffeta*

1926	July	Ruth Manning-Sanders, *Martha-Wish-You-Ill*
	July	Edwin Muir, *Chorus of the Newly Dead*
	October	Stanley Snaith, *April Morning*
1927	November	Laura Riding, *Voltaire*
1928	June	Stanley Snaith, *A Flying Scroll*
1930	November	Virginia Woolf, *On Being Ill*
1931	July	V. Sackville-West, *Sissinghurst*
	December	George Rylands, *Poems*
1932	May	Dorothy Wellesley, *Jupiter and the Nun*

Appendix B

List of Handprinted Books in Order by Author

Bell, Clive	*Poems* (1921) *The Legend of Monte Della Sibilla* (1923)
Bosanquet, Theodora	*Henry James at Work* (1924)
Cunard, Nancy	*Parallax* (1925)
Eliot, T. S.	*Poems* (1919) *The Waste Land* (1923)
Forster, E. M.	*The Story of the Siren* (1920) *Pharos and Pharillon* (1923)
Fry, Roger	*Twelve Original Woodcuts* (1921)
Graves, Robert	*The Feather Bed* (1923)
Limebeer, Ena	*To a Proud Phantom* (1923)
Manning-Sanders, Ruth	*Karn* (1923) *Martha-Wish-You-Ill* (1926)
Mansfield, Katherine	*Prelude* (1918)
Mirrlees, Hope	*Paris* (1920)
Muir, Edwin	*Chorus of the Newly Dead* (1926)
Palmer, Herbert E.	*Songs of Salvation, Sin, and Satire* (1925)
Prewitt, Frank	*Poems* (1921)
Ransom, John Crowe	*Grace after Meat* (1924)

Read, Herbert	*Mutations of the Phoenix* (1923)
Riding, Laura	*Voltaire* (1927)
Rylands, George	*Russet and Taffeta* (1925) *Poems* (1931)
Sackville-West, V.	*Sissinghurst* (1931)
Shove, Fredegond	*Daybreak* (1922)
Snaith, Stanley	*April Morning* (1926) *A Flying Scroll* (1928)
Trevelyan, R. C.	*Poems and Fables* (1925)
Wellesley, Dorothy	*Jupiter and the Nun* (1932)
Woolf, C. N. Sidney	*Poems* (1918)
Woolf, Leonard	*Two Stories* (1917) *Stories of the East* (1921)
Woolf, Virginia	*Two Stories* (1917) *Kew Gardens* (1919) *On Being Ill* (1930)

Notes

Chapter 1

1. Leonard Woolf, *Beginning Again* (London: Hogarth Press, 1963), p. 231.

2. George Spater and Ian Parsons, *A Marriage of True Minds: An Intimate Portrait of Leonard and Virginia Woolf* (New York: Harcourt, Brace, Jovanovich, 1977), p. 4.

3. L. Woolf, *Beginning*, pp. 9–14.

4. Ibid., 231–55.

5. Spater and Parsons, *Marriage*, p. 107. Ralph Partridge (1920–23), Marjorie Joad (1923–25), G. W. Rylands (July–December, 1924), Angus Davidson (1924–27), Bernadette Murphy (February–July, 1925), Mrs. Cartwright (1925–30), Richard Kennedy (1930–31), John Lehmann (1931–32, 1938–46).

6. Ibid., pp. 107–8.

7. Stanley B. Olsen, "The History of The Hogarth Press: 1917–1923; A Biographical Study, with Critical Discussion of Selected Publications" (Ph.D. dissertation, University of London, 1972), pp. 21–22.

8. *The Complete Catalogue of the Hogarth Press* (London: Hogarth Press, 1939).

9. L. Woolf, *Beginning*, p. 29.

10. Spater and Parsons, *Marriage*, p. 163.

11. Leonard Woolf, *Sowing* (London: Hogarth Press, 1960), p. 12.

12. Virginia Woolf, *A Writer's Diary* (London: Hogarth Press, 1953), p. 328.

13. Virginia Woolf, *The Diary of Virginia Woolf, Volume III, 1925–1930* (New York: Harcourt, Brace, Jovanovich, 1980), p. 126, note 1.

Chapter 2

1. Peter Stansky, "Leonard Woolf's Journey," *Atlantic*, May, 1970, p. 118; Spater and Parsons, *Marriage*, p. 175.

2. Leonard Woolf, *Downhill All the Way* (London: Hogarth Press, 1967), p. 70.

3. Dora Carrington, *Letters and Extracts from Her Diary*, chosen by David Garnett (New York: Holt, Rinehart, and Winston, 1979); Noel Carrington, *Carrington: Paintings, Drawings and Decorations* (New York, Thames and Hudson, 1980); Richard Shone, *Bloomsbury Portraits* (New York: Dutton, 1976).

Chapter 3

1. Virginia Woolf, *The Letters of Virginia Woolf Volume II, 1912–1922* (New York: Harcourt, Brace, Jovanovich, 1978), p. 581: 7? November 1922.

2. L. Woolf, *Beginning*, p. 242.

3. V. Woolf, *Diary, Volume I*, 19 March 1919.

4. V. Woolf, *Letters, Volume III*, to Barbara Hiles Bagenal, 24 June 1923.

5. Olsen, *History*, p. 37.

6. V. Woolf, *Diary, Volume II*, 12 April 1921.

7. Olsen, *History*, pp. 27–28.

8. Donald A. Laing, *Roger Fry, An Annotated Bibliography of Published Writings* (New York: Garland Press, 1979), p. 232.

9. Richard Shone, *Bloomsbury Portraits: Vanessa Bell, Duncan Grant and Their Circle* (New York: E.P. Dutton, 1976), p. 170.

10. Mary E. Gaither, "The Hogarth Press: 1917–1938," in J. Howard Woolmer, *A Checklist of The Hogarth Press, 1917–1938* (Andes, New York: Woolmer, Brotherson Ltd., 1976), p. 17.

11. Quentin Bell, *Virginia Woolf, A Biography, Volume II* (New York: Harcourt, Brace, Jovanovich, 1972), p. 50.

12. V. Woolf, *Diary, Volume II*, 23 June 1922.

13. V. Woolf, *Letters, Volume II*, to Vanessa Bell, 19 December 1917.

14. L. Woolf, *Beginning*, p. 182.

Chapter 4

1. V. Woolf, *Letters, Volume IV*, to Theodora Bosanquet, 7 November 1929.

2. V. Woolf, *Letters, Volume III*, to Gerald Brenan, December 1923.

3. Leon Edel, *Henry James, Volume V, 1901–1916: The Master* (Philadelphia: Lippincott, 1972), p. 360.

4. V. Woolf, *Letters, Volume III*, to Theodora Bosanquet, 24 February 1924.

5. Hugh Ford, ed., *Nancy Cunard, Brave Poet, Indomitable Rebel* (Philadelphia: Chilton Books, 1968), p. 69.

6. V. Woolf, *Diary, Volume III*, 27 April 1925.

7. V. Woolf, *Letters, Volume II*, to Dora Carrington, 24 August 1922: "Captain Graves, the poet Graves, wants us to print a poem, with a portrait by Eric Kennington—who is he?" The note identifies this poem as *The Feather Bed*.

8. V. Woolf, *Letters, Volume III*, to Gerald Brenan, 12 May 1923.

9. V. Woolf, *Letters, Volume II*, to Lytton Strachey, 25 July 1916.

10. For this story from Alix Strachey and related ones about the Press from Barbara Begenal, Angus Davidson, Ralph Partridge and George Rylands, see Joan Russell Noble, ed., *Recollections of Virginia Woolf* (New York: William Morrow, 1972).

11. L. Woolf, *Beginning*, p. 237.

12. Woolmer, *Checklist*, pp. 31 and 155.

13. L. Woolf, *Downhill*, p. 67.

14. Olsen, *History*, p. 33.

15. V. Woolf, *Diary, Volume I*, 3 September 1918; Olsen, *History*, p. 33.

16. L. Woolf, *Downhill*, pp. 131-32.

17. V. Woolf, *Letters, Volume III*, to V. Sackville-West, 5 January 1926.

Chapter 5

1. L. Woolf, *Downhill*, pp. 65, 77.

2. Olsen, *History*, p. 33.

3. Victoria Glendinning, *Vita: The Life of V. Sackville-West* (New York: Knopf, 1983), p. 240.

4. For information on Prewitt, see the writings of Lady Ottoline Morrell and Siegfried Sassoon.

5. I have discovered that the Georgian poet Ralph Hodgson started a poetry sheet called the *Flying Scroll* but I did not discover any connection with Snaith; perhaps he was also supported by Edward Marsh and that forms a connection.

Chapter 6

1. L. Woolf, *Beginning*, p. 234.

2. Roderick Cave, *The Private Press* (New York: Watson-Guptill, 1971), p. 200.

3. Colin Franklin, *The Private Presses* (Chester Springs, Pa.: Dufour, 1969), p. 121.

4. John Lehmann, *Thrown to the Woolfs* (New York: Holt, Rinehart and Winston, 1978), p. 5.

5. Cave, *Private Press*, p. 201.

6. Douglas C. McMurtrie, *The Book, The Story of Printing and Bookmaking* (New York: Oxford University Press, 1967), p. 473.

7. Woolmer, *Checklist*, p. 7.

Bibliography

Primary Sources

Bell, Clive. *The Legend of Monte della Sibilla or Le Paradis de la Reine Sibille*. Richmond: Hogarth Press, 1923.
_____. *Poems*. Richmond: Hogarth Press, 1921.
Bosanquet, Theodora. *Henry James at Work*. London: Hogarth Press, 1924.
Carrington, Dora. *Carrington: Letters and Extracts from Her Diaries Chosen and with an Introduction by David Garnett*. New York: Holt, Rinehart, and Winston, 1970.
Cunard, Nancy. *Parallax*. London: Hogarth Press, 1925.
Eliot, T.S. *Poems*. Richmond: Hogarth Press, 1919.
_____. *The Waste Land*. Richmond: Hogarth Press, 1923.
Forster, E.M. *Pharos and Pharillon*. Richmond: Hogarth Press, 1923.
_____. *The Story of the Siren*. Richmond: Hogarth Press, 1920.
Fry, Roger. *Letters of Roger Fry*. Edited with an introduction by Denys Sutton. New York: Random House, 1972.
_____. *Twelve Original Woodcuts*. Richmond: Hogarth Press, 1921.
Garnett, David. *The Golden Echo*. London: Chatto and Windus, 1970.
Graves, Robert. *The Feather Bed*. Richmond: Hogarth Press, 1923.
_____. *Good-Bye to All That: An Autobiography*. Garden City, New York: Doubleday, Anchor, 1929, 1957.
Lehmann, John. *In My Own Time*. Boston: Atlantic/Little Brown, 1969.
_____. *Thrown to the Woolfs: Leonard and Virginia Woolf and the Hogarth Press*. New York: Holt, Rinehart and Winston, 1979.
Limebeer, Ena. *To a Proud Phantom*. Richmond: Hogarth Press, 1923.
Manning-Sanders, Ruth. *Karn*. Richmond: Hogarth Press, 1922.
_____. *Martha-Wish-You-Ill*. London: Hogarth Press, 1926.
Mansfield, Katherine. *The Journal of Katherine Mansfield*. Edited by J.M. Murry. New York: Alfred A. Knopf, 1927.
_____. *The Letters of Katherine Mansfield*. Edited by J. Middleton Murry. New York: Alfred A. Knopf, 1929.
_____. *Prelude*. Richmond: Hogarth Press, 1918.
Mirrlees, Hope. *Paris: A Poem*. Richmond: Hogarth Press, 1919.
Morrell, Ottoline. *Memoirs of Lady Ottoline Morrell: A Study in Friendship, 1873-1915*. Edited by Robert Garthorne-Hardy. New York: Alfred A. Knopf, 1964.
_____. *Ottoline at Garsington: Memoirs of Lady Ottoline Morrell, 1915-1918*. Edited by Robert Garthorne-Hardy. New York: Alfred A. Knopf, 1975.

Muir, Edwin. *Chorus of the Newly Dead.* London: Hogarth Press, 1926.

Palmer, Herbert E. *Songs of Salvation, Sin and Satire.* London: Hogarth Press, 1925.

Prewitt, Frank. *Poems.* Richmond: Hogarth Press, 1921.

Ransom, John Crowe. *Grace after Meat.* London: Hogarth Press, 1924.

Read, Herbert. *Mutations of the Phoenix.* Richmond: Hogarth Press, 1923.

Riding, Laura. *Voltaire: A Biographical Fantasy.* London: Hogarth Press, 1927.

Rylands, George. *Poems.* London: Hogarth Press, 1931.

_____. *Russet and Taffeta.* London: Hogarth Press, 1925.

Sackville-West, V. *Sissinghurst.* London: Hogarth Press, 1931.

Sassoon, Siegfried. *Siegfried Sassoon, Diaries, Nineteen Fifteen to Nineteen Eighteen.* Boston: Faber and Faber, 1983.

_____. *Siegfried Sassoon, Diaries, Nineteen Twenty to Nineteen Twenty-Two.* Boston: Faber and Faber, 1983.

Shove, Fredegond. *Daybreak.* Richmond. Hogarth Press, 1922.

Snaith, Stanley. *April Morning.* London: Hogarth Press, 1926.

_____. *A Flying Scroll.* London: Hogarth Press, 1928.

Trevelyan, R.C. *Poems and Fables.* London: Hogarth Press, 1925.

Wellesley, Dorothy. *Jupiter and the Nun.* London: Hogarth Press, 1932.

Woolf, C.N. Sidney. *Poems.* Richmond: Hogarth Press, 1918.

Woolf, Leonard. *Beginning Again: An Autobiography of the Years 1911 to 1918.* London: Hogarth Press, 1963.

_____. *Downhill All the Way: An Autobiography of the Years 1919–1939.* London: Hogarth Press, 1967.

_____. *Growing: An Autobiography of the Years 1904–1911.* London: Hogarth Press, 1961.

_____. *The Journey Not the Arrival: An Autobiography of the Years 1939–1969.* London: Hogarth Press, 1969.

_____. *Sowing: An Autobiography of the Years 1880–1904.* London: Hogarth Press, 1960.

_____. *Stories of the East.* Richmond: Hogarth Press, 1921.

Woolf, Leonard and Virginia. *Two Stories.* Richmond: Hogarth Press, 1917.

Woolf, Virginia. *The Diary of Virginia Woolf: Volume I, 1915–1919.* Edited by Olivier Bell. New York: Harcourt, Brace, Jovanovich, 1977.

_____. *The Diary of Virginia Woolf: Volume II, 1920–1924.* Edited by Olivier Bell. New York: Harcourt, Brace, Jovanovich, 1978.

_____. *The Diary of Virginia Woolf: Volume III, 1925–1930.* Edited by Olivier Bell. New York: Harcourt, Brace, Jovanovich, 1980.

_____. *The Diary of Virginia Woolf: Volume IV, 1931–1935.* Edited by Olivier Bell. New York: Harcourt, Brace, Jovanovich, 1982.

_____. *Kew Gardens.* Richmond: Hogarth Press, 1919.

_____. *Letters of Virginia Woolf: Volume I, 1888–1912.* Edited by Nigel Nicolson and Joanne Trautmann. New York: Harcourt, Brace, Jovanovich, 1977.

_____. *Letters of Virginia Woolf: Volume II, 1912–1922.* Edited by Nigel Nicolson and Joanne Trautmann. New York: Harcourt, Brace, Jovanovich, 1978.

_____. *Letters of Virginia Woolf: Volume III, 1923–1928.* Edited by Nigel Nicolson and Joanne Trautmann. New York: Harcourt, Brace, Jovanovich, 1979.

_____. *Letters of Virginia Woolf: Volume IV, 1929–1931.* Edited by Nigel Nicolson and Joanne Trautmann. New York: Harcourt, Brace, Jovanovich, 1979.

_____. *Letters of Virginia Woolf: Volume V, 1932–1935.* Edited by Nigel Nicolson and Joanne Trautmann. New York: Harcourt, Brace, Jovanovich, 1980.

_____. *Letters of Virginia Woolf: Volume VI, 1936–1941.* Edited by Nigel Nicolson and Joanne Trautmann. New York: Harcourt, Brace, Jovanovich, 1980.

_____. *On Being Ill.* London: Hogarth Press, 1930.

_____. *A Writer's Diary: Being Extracts from the Diary of Virginia Woolf.* Edited by Leonard Woolf. London: Hogarth Press, 1959.

Secondary Sources

Alpers, Anthony. *The Life of Katherine Mansfield.* New York: Penguin Books, 1982.

Anscombe, Isabelle. *Omega and After: Bloomsbury and the Decorative Arts.* New York: Thames and Hudson, 1981.

Art of the Printed Book 1455-1955; Masterpieces of Typography through Five Centuries from the Collection of the Pierpont Morgan Library. New York, Boston: David R. Godine, 1973.

Bell, Alan. "The Development of a Diversion," *Times Literary Supplement,* 25 July 1975, p. 822.

Bell, Quentin. *Bloomsbury.* London: Weidenfeld and Nicolson, 1968.

_____. *Virginia Woolf: A Biography.* New York: Harcourt, Brace, Jovanovich, 1972.

The Bloomsbury Group, A Collection of Memoirs, Commentary and Criticism. Edited by S.P. Rosenbaum. Toronto: University of Toronto Press, 1975.

Brabazon, James. *Dorothy L. Sayers.* New York: Avon Books, 1981.

Carrington, Nocl. *Carrington: Paintings, Drawings and Decorations.* New York: Thames and Hudson, 1980.

Carter, John. *ABC for Book Collectors.* London: Hart-Davis, 1974.

Catalogue of Books from the Library of Leonard and Virginia Woolf: Taken from Monks House, Rodmell, Sussex and 24 Victoria Square, London and Now in the Possession of Washington State University, Pullman. Brighton, England: Holleyman and Treacher, n.d.

Cave, Roderick. *The Private Press.* New York: Watson-Guptill, 1971.

Darroch, Sandra Jobson. *Ottoline, The Life of Lady Ottoline Morrell.* New York: Coward, McCann and Geoghegan, 1975.

Edel, Leon. *Bloomsbury, A House of Lions.* Philadelphia: J.B. Lippincott, 1979.

_____. *The Life of Henry James, Volume V, The Master.* Philadelphia: Lippincott, 1972.

Edmiston, Susan. "The Bookmaking of Virginia and Leonard Woolf." *Craft Horizon* 34 (August 1974), pp. 24-25.

Ellman, Richard, ed. *The Norton Anthology of Modern Poetry.* New York: W. W. Norton, 1973.

Farr, Dennis. *English Art 1870-1940.* Oxford: Oxford University Press, 1978.

Franklin, Colin. *The Private Presses.* Chester Springs, Pa.: Dufour Editions, 1969.

Ford, Hugh, ed. *Nancy Cunard: Brave Poet, Indomitable Rebel.* Philadelphia: Chilton Books, 1968.

Furbank, P. N. *E. M. Forster: A Life.* New York: Harcourt, Brace, Jovanovich, 1978.

Fussell, Paul. *The Great War and Modern Memory.* Oxford: Oxford University Press, 1975.

Gadd, David. *The Loving Friends: A Portrait of Bloomsbury.* New York: Harcourt, Brace, Jovanovich, 1974.

Gardner, Brian, ed. *Up the Line to Death—The War Poets 1914-1918; An Anthology Selected and Arranged, with an Introduction and Notes by Brian Gardner.* New York: Clarkson N. Potter, 1967.

Glendinning, Victoria. *Vita: The Life of V. Sackville-West.* New York: Alfred A. Knopf, 1983.

Hamilton, Ian. "Graves and Goddesses." *New York Review of Books,* 18 August 1983, pp. 38-41.

Heilbrun, Carolyn G., ed. *Lady Ottoline's Album: Snapshots and Portraits of Her Famous Contemporaries (and of Herself) Photographed for the Most Part by Lady Ottoline Morrell.* New York: Alfred A. Knopf, 1976.

The Hogarth Press: Complete Catalogue of Publications Arranged under Subjects to the Summer of 1939. London: Hogarth Press, 1939.

Holroyd, Michael. *Lytton Strachey: A Critical Biography.* New York: Holt, Rinehart and Winston, 1968. 2 vols.

Kennedy, Richard. *A Boy at the Hogarth Press.* New York: Heinemann, 1972.

Kramer, Hilton. "Bloomsbury Idols." *The New Criterion* (January 1984), pp. 1–9.

Laing, Donald A. *Roger Fry, An Annotated Bibliography of the Published Writings.* New York: Garland Publishing, 1979.

Lehmann, John. *Virginia Woolf and Her World.* New York: Harcourt, Brace, Jovanovich, 1975.

Lehmann, John, ed. *English Poets of the First World War.* New York: Thames and Hudson, 1982.

Levy, Paul. *Moore: G. E. Moore and the Cambridge Apostles.* New York: Holt, Rinehart, and Winston, 1979.

Luedeking, Leica. "Bibliography of Works by Leonard S. Woolf." *Virginia Woolf Quarterly* 1 (1972), pp. 120–40.

Mathews, Harry. "Queen Story." *New York Review of Books,* 29 April 1982, pp. 37–42.

McMurtrie, Douglas C. *The Book, the Story of Printing and Bookmaking.* New York: Oxford University Press, 1967.

Meyerowitz, Selma. "The Hogarth Letters: Bloomsbury Writers on Art and Politics." *San Jose Studies* 5:i, pp. 76–85.

Mumby, Frank Arthur and Ian Norrie. *Publishing and Bookselling.* London: Jonathan Cape, 1974.

Nicolson, Nigel. *Portrait of a Marriage: V. Sackville-West and Harold Nicolson.* New York: Atheneum, 1973.

Noble, Joan Russell, ed. *Recollections of Virginia Woolf.* New York: William Morrow, 1972.

Olsen, Stanley B. "The History of the Hogarth Press: 1917–1923; A Biographical Study, with Critical Discussion of Selected Publications." Ph.D. dissertation, University of London, 1972.

Plomer, William. *Electric Delights.* Boston: David R. Godine, 1978.

Sencourt, Robert. *T. S. Eliot: A Memoir.* New York: Dell Publishing, 1971.

Shone, Richard. *Bloomsbury Portraits: Vanessa Bell, Duncan Grant and Their Circle.* New York: E. P. Dutton, 1976.

———. *The Century of Change: British Painting since 1900.* New York: E. P. Dutton, 1977.

Spalding, Frances. *Roger Fry: Art and Life.* Berkeley: University of California Press, 1980.

———. *Vanessa Bell.* New Haven: Ticknor and Fields, 1983.

Spater, George, and Ian Parsons. *A Marriage of True Minds: An Intimate Portrait of Leonard and Virginia Woolf.* New York: Harcourt, Brace, Jovanovich, 1977.

Stansky, Peter. "Leonard Woolf's Journey." *Atlantic,* May 1970, pp. 116–19.

Sutherland, J. A. *Victorian Novelists and Publishers.* Chicago: University of Chicago Press, 1976.

Swinnerton, Frank. *The Georgian Scene, A Literary Panorama.* New York: Farrar and Rinehart, 1934.

Tindall, William York. *Forces in Modern British Literature 1885–1946.* New York: Alfred A. Knopf, 1979.

University of Chicago Press. *A Manual of Style: Containing Typographical and Other Rules for Authors, Printers and Publishers Recommended by the University of Chicago Press Together with Specimens of Type.* Chicago: The University of Chicago Press, 1961.

Wilson, Duncan. *Leonard Woolf: A Political Biography.* New York: St. Martin's, 1978.

Woolf, Virginia. *Roger Fry: A Biography.* London: The Hogarth Press, 1940.

Woolmer, J. Howard. *A Checklist of the Hogarth Press, 1917–1938.* With a short history of the press by Mary E. Gaither. Andes, New York: Woolmer and Brotherson, Ltd., 1976.

Yeats, William Butler, ed. *The Oxford Book of Modern Verse, 1892–1935.* Oxford: Oxford University Press, 1936.

Index